By the same author:

Short and Shorter Stories for Adults
Short Stories for Children
Once Upon A Long Time Ago
Nursery Rhymes
Once Upon A Younger World
The Complete Works of My Kind of Poetry
Fun Quizzes

ANIMALS, PETS AND ME
AND
FEATHERS, SPIKES AND FUR

Gisela D. Pilot

Book Guild Publishing
Sussex, England

First published in Great Britain in 2014 by
The Book Guild Ltd
The Werks
45 Church Road
Hove, BN3 2BE

Typesetting in Garamond by
Keyboard Services, Luton, Bedfordshire

Printed and bound in Croatia under the supervision of
MRM Graphics Ltd, Winslow, Bucks

A catalogue record for this book is available from
The British Library

ISBN 978 1 909984 40 0

Contents

Animals, Pets And Me

My earliest recollection is being dragged along by my mother, to the loud wailing of sirens which hurt my ears so. In my left hand I clutched a small, knitted animal. It dropped out of my hand. Somehow I wrenched my hand out of my mother's and ran back to retrieve my treasured possession. As I did so, it and I were scooped up by a strong pair of arms. Seconds later something dropped out of the sky and hit the ground, just where I had dropped my 'pet'.

In the mid- to late 1980s, while visiting my parents in Pembrokeshire, we started reminiscing about our lives in Germany, and I brought my earliest memory into the conversation. Both looked at each other in disbelief, shaking their heads violently, insisting that there was no way I could have remembered that incident since I was barely two and a half years old at the time. But yes, it was towards the end of the war, and yes, a stray cigar-shaped bomb had dropped, as I had said, and fortunately, not exploded. It was only after I told my mother that she had worn a green dress that she sat agape and wide-eyed and finally conceded that the event had happened as I had described.

Sometime later, and I don't know whether it was weeks or months (nor do I recall where my two sisters, six and seven years older than me, were at that time), my mother and I were staying with my grandmother. She had been a housekeeper in a doctor's large house where she occupied two attic rooms in her semi-retirement.

It was from there that I heard a strange sound early one morning. I clambered up onto piles of stuff on top of a chest, in order to see out of the window. There, way down below, through the gaps between branches and leaves, I saw soldiers

3

marching on shiny black cobbles which glistened from the night's drizzle. The sound made by all those hobnailed boots fascinated me.

Again, there seems to be a time lapse but while staying at grandmother's another time, a circus came to town. The parade of clowns, big cats, monkeys, horses, fire-eaters, people on stilts and huge elephants with big, flapping ears passed by. I noticed that one of the great grey beasts was different from the other four. It had five legs! The fifth was quite short and thinner than its other two legs at the back. Well into my adulthood, at a Showmen's Guild dinner dance to which we had been invited, I related my five-legged elephant story to a one-time circus performer. He assured me that the 'bull' elephant would have only taken part in the parade purely for exercise. Other than that he was a working animal, helping to lift and move things.

In the afternoon my parents (I don't know where my father had been or come from to join us, and still no sign of my sisters) and I went to the Big Top.

We were halfway up the tiered seats. I stood between my parents, jumping from foot to foot, squealing with delight at all that was going on down there on the thick layers of golden sawdust. All the clowns and the animals I had seen that morning were there, the animals performing to the commands of their trainers. I didn't see the elephant with three legs at the back again, though.

The people sitting around us applauded as they watched me clapping in my obvious sheer delight at the goings-on. Perhaps my enthusiasm got the better of me, for I may have fallen asleep, as I cannot remember leaving the Big Top or where we went from there.

My father was a meteorologist during the war. Much later I was told that he had been excellent in his field, so much so that the Russians wanted him and pursued him when he was on his way home, just as peace had been declared.

Both my sisters had reappeared. We were playing outside while a large van was being packed with all our things. We saw our father haring up the road. He called to my mother with utmost urgency in his voice. She appeared, carrying a big bag, and we ran in what we stood up in, as fast as we could.

For how long we were on the run, I don't know. I remember my father exchanging his uniform with the clothes of scarecrows. I remember eating and drinking in a few cafés along the way. I also recall a farmer giving us a lift in a wagon and sleeping in haystacks.

Thus we arrived in the little village of Bensen, about five miles from Hamlin. We had pilfered a set of cutlery, a cup, a saucer and plate along the way, from the cafés we had stopped at.

Father left us outside a big front yard with tall brick pillars either side of the entrance to a farm. Soon after, he returned with the farmer, who greeted us warmly and bade us welcome. We were introduced to his wife and ushered into an enormous kitchen where we sat at an equally enormous wooden table. In next to no time, food, coffee and beakers of fresh milk were served and ravenously scoffed. Hungry no more, and my thirst quenched, I think I must have fallen asleep, only to be rudely awoken, stripped naked and washed from head to toe under cold running water. Enough to give a robust child of more advanced years a heart attack, let alone a little biddy like me.

While we had eaten and bathed, a large, square room had been got ready for us. In it was a massive bed, a couple of armchairs, a cot, a cupboard, a chest of drawers, a table and five chairs. The farmer and my dad had served together, and he had said to my father, 'If ever...'

The rest is history. So, this was it! This was home now!

The bed was, at least, king-sized but after several nights of two adults and two children sharing it, another bedroom was created. Coming in from the yard, up some steps, through the heavy wooden front door into a big hall, the door to our room was the first on the left. There were other doors, too, and at the end of the spacious hall, in the left-hand corner, steps led up to an attic. A number of bales of hay had been loosened and padded into a mattress. With several sheets and blankets it became a soft, cosy and warm bed for three little girls.

Life on the farm was always hectic and people only got together at mealtimes unless they were working in fields away from the farm. There were horses, cows, a few sheep and goats, a couple of dogs and poultry.

One morning all the farmhands were assembled out in the yard and listened to a pep talk. The farmer spoke in his usual calm voice, congratulating everybody for the fine work they were doing, and asking them to, please, continue in like fashion, all working together for the same good.

I took on board that everybody had to pitch in. Surely I was one of 'everybody' and I, too, wanted to help. Later that morning I went to the cowshed. Coming in from the sunshine I had to blink and rub my eyes a few times to adjust to the dark barn. I saw the milking stool as I had seen, being used, before. I found a bucket, too. It was quite heavy for me but I managed to carry it and placed it, strategically, under the first of the six cows in their stalls.

I sat on the stool and got hold of the teat nearest to me. I nearly lost my balance, and held on tightly to the teats which saved me from toppling over. Still hanging on, I sat square on the stool again.

Right. Ready! Without warning the bucket was kicked, and it rolled towards the front legs of the cow. I held on even tighter to my anchor and it was then that the cow's tail swished across the left side of my face, plastering me with wet dung. I was mortified. My pride was hurt. All I had wanted to do was to be useful and help out! My milking days came to an abrupt end.

There was a water tap and hose nearby with a zinc bath under it. I washed my face and my hair on my left side. I wandered back out into the sunshine and played by myself, as usual, and explored the nooks and crannies of the yard.

My father helped in all sorts of ways on the farm and in the fields. He was born and brought up on a smallholding, so he felt quite at home. He helped out on other farms, too, and in the village as and when and where things needed doing. His pay was as varied as the jobs. A bag of flour or sugar. A bucket of fruit. A sack of potatoes. Vegetables. Sausages or meat from a recent slaughter.

As well as some food he came home one day with a wooden Dachshund on four wheels. His tail was hooked onto the hind legs and back of the dog; the middle hinged to the back and to the shoulders and front legs. The head was secured to the front of the body. Between the front legs was a looped screw through which a string had been threaded. I was the proud owner of my very own dog! As I pulled him, his tail would wag and his body would twist this way and that. I loved my Dackel and we walked everywhere together. He was my best friend. My only friend at that time. I always seemed to get in someone's way and was always told 'Go and play'. I often would talk to Dackel and was glad to get something off my little chest. I swear he understood my every word.

One day we had walked across the yard almost to the brick pillars, beyond which I was not allowed to go. Just this side of the left pillar lay a huge boulder, three-quarters surrounded by stinging nettles. I clambered up the nettle-free side with Dackel in tow and sat on the stone, which had been warmed by the sun.

Next door was a small cottage which belonged to the farm. There lived a refugee family with two daughters and a son. The boy, about seven or eight, with ginger hair and big freckles on his face, slunk around the pillar and cockily asked me my name. He asked what I had in my arms. He laughed a dirty, knowing laugh, pointed and said that Dackel wasn't a proper dog. I wanted to cry but pressed my lips together as tightly as I could. The lad came closer. His grubby hands reached towards us. I cringed, pulled back and cuddled Dackel even closer as we rolled off the boulder into a dense bed of nettles. Now I cried! No, I screamed and screamed! A number of people rushed towards the screaming and before I knew it I had been stripped of my pants and little summer dress and I was sitting in the zinc bath full of cold water, in the cowshed – still screaming!

For the next few years I so hated that kid next door. He left a lasting impression on me. I have never, to this day, liked ginger or red hair, or freckles, come to that.

One day, everyone had returned from the fields. One of the horses, too, had made it back to the yard where it promptly collapsed and died. I had never seen a dead anything before and didn't really register what had happened. People were running around. In time, several men came, official-looking men. With much effort and a lot of pushing, pulling and heaving, the horse was rolled onto a large, green sheet and covered up. The next day the butcher got to work. That Sunday, everybody in the village had a roast dinner.

There was a house back up the road which had been hit by lightning some time before our arrival and suffered quite a lot of damage. Everyone pitched in, as and when they had the time. While the building and renovating took place, Dad came home with a gorgeous golden-haired dog one day. She couldn't live on the farm with us so Father built a wooden kennel for Senta and she guarded the house, not that anything needed guarding in those days.

Somehow one of Dad's legs was injured. He could hardly walk. He got a tall tin of food ready for the dog. The tin had two holes around the top with string for a carrying handle through them. I was to take the tin, to feed Senta. Right on the top lay a dead mouse! I screamed and dropped the tin. My father gathered up the food, including the offending corpse and hobbled, in much pain, the quarter of a mile to the house, using me as a stabiliser. From a little way off. Dad tossed the mouse towards Senta who deftly caught it, and it never even touched the sides!

My mother earned her crust by sewing, crocheting, darning, embroidery, tapestry, mending and knitting. She had always been an excellent needlewoman from a very young age. Word soon got around, and besides mending linen and work clothes for the farm she was hardly ever without needles of some sort. This is where Dackel and I came into our own. We sometimes had to pick up wool or material or deliver a finished article to someone somewhere in the neighbourhood. We were, by this time, allowed outside the great portals.

The following spring we moved into our house. It stood in a large plot of land, the soil of which was quickly dug and raked, seeded and planted.

The door was at the back. Just inside was the wash-kitchen on the left. Opposite this, two steps led down into the kitchen with a cast iron stove, a pantry, some shelves, table and chairs, a bench and a cupboard. All but the stove and pantry had come with us from the farm. At the end of the passage to the right was a very big, square room with a floor-to-ceiling cast iron and part-tiled stove. A big table, six chairs, and the massive bed from the farm, furnished the lounge. From there, a door and stairs led up to the only bedroom.

The end of the passage was boarded up. Behind this was the rest of the house where yet another refugee family lived with three children, all quite a few years older than my sisters.

Senta went walkabout one day, exploring her new surroundings, now that she was no longer on a chain. We could hear her barking excitedly. Dad called her. He whistled. Nothing. Then we heard a painful yelp. We ran down the path between us and the farm next door. Across the grassy field, by a fence, lay Senta, dead. Dad carried her limp body back up the lane with tears glistening in his eyes.

Apparently she had chased some geese and somebody had given her a whack across her back, breaking it. I don't know how or who but sometime later her tanned, beautiful, soft coat lay on the floor in the lounge, in front of the big bed.

We were separated from our neighbours the other side, by a long, barn-like building. Our neighbour's husband had not returned from the war. She had two sons. As she had spare rooms upstairs she had had to take in a widow and her three children, two girls and a boy. He and one of his sisters were twins. Those three and the older boy downstairs were the same sort of age as my sisters. The small son was a year younger than me.

Great commotion. They had all been playing out in the front and then came running home, reporting a stray pig wandering down the main road, which was no more than a dirt track. With a belt around its neck, my father detained the pig while we all ran in different directions asking everybody if they had lost a pig. A resounding no, all round.

Going from the wash-kitchen out to the side, my father built an outside toilet. The finishing touches completed and the door hung, we just had to wait for the mortar to dry.

Unceremoniously the pig was led, coaxed and pulled the 50-odd yards to the side of our house and pushed into the newly built outside loo. Pig didn't like that! It squealed, deafening squeals, and kicked and kicked to find a way out. That wasn't too difficult a task as the cement was still wet. Any one of us could have leant against either side wall which would quite easily have given way. With an ear-piercing squeal and a kick up its backside from my dad, the pig ran off, heard for quite a while, but never to be seen again!

All of us helped to gather the bricks and tidy up, and in no time, with a few choice expletives muttered under his breath, my father soon made good the damage and eventually was the first to christen the new outhouse known as 'The Pigsty'. Any thoughts of months of roast pork, bacon, sausages, black pudding, trotters or brawn had long been forgotten.

Peter, my little friend from next door, and I often went exploring. The wire fence at the end of our garden backed onto the path from the back of his house. This led down a rough, stony slope, with elder bushes either side, almost as far down as the little stream. The grass field to the left, the field where Senta had lain dead, had three rows of electric fence running between posts right across to the other side of the stream, and then left from there to the back of one of next door's farm buildings. At the bottom of the path just inside the fence, we found four big eggs one day. We gathered them up, two each, and took them home. Things were hard to get in those days and nobody asked us how we had come by them.

Another day, down by the stream again, we heard a lot of humming and buzzing. We looked around and then up. In a tree just the other side of the stream hung a huge ball that seemed to be alive. We picked a few stones out of the water and threw them towards the buzzing mass. The stones only reached a few feet above the ground and were no threat to the humming ball. We quickly realised what the ball was, and legged it home. A couple of the older children were dispatched on bikes to the next village. Not long after a beekeeper, suitably attired and carrying a smoke puffer, came and thankfully gathered his swarm. A few days later he and his wife came with pots of honey for us all.

Dad came home another time with his pay packet, a big, black, shiny, silky-haired rabbit – for the pot. It was Friday. The next day, Dad was to kill the rabbit ready for Sunday. Overnight the big, fat buck turned into a doe and gave birth to six baby rabbits! We had vegetable soup for Sunday dinner.

By this time we had also acquired some chickens, and ended up with one each. The one my mother claimed as hers followed her about everywhere. Mum was in the kitchen one day when suddenly she nearly jumped out of her skin. Her chicken cackled for all it was worth as it stood up and flapped its wings triumphantly. It has laid an egg in my mother's round sewing basket. This became quite a regular occurrence.

The girls and their peers were outside and called for me to come out, 'Quickly!' My older sister had hold of my chicken. She wedged it under my left arm and told me it was about to lay an egg. 'You can feel it!' While they all ran off, laughing hysterically, I was left clutching my very irate chicken with one of my fingers up its backside. No, don't laugh! It wasn't funny! I didn't think so, anyway and I don't think my chicken was highly amused either. Nor had I felt an egg.

In front of Peter's house stood a tall old pear tree, dripping with delicious ripe fruit. We had already eaten a couple of pears each. A lot had dropped and lay splattered on the ground. It was late summer and the place was buzzing, a familiar sound to us. I was taking a last bite when I stepped onto a squashed pear, already occupied by a wasp. In its defence it promptly stung me. Of course I screamed out. Just then my father came round the comer with a spade, rake and hoe over one shoulder. Across the road was a barren field, parts of which were allowed to be cultivated by anyone inclined to do so. Although we had a big vegetable garden ourselves, a small patch of this field had been put to good use. I hobbled alongside Dad, still sobbing and feeling sorry for myself. I had been stung under my left sole, so I painfully balanced along on tiptoe. When we reached the field. Dad turned over some of the rich, black soil and told me to step in it. It felt so cool and seemed to soothe my foot. He picked me a few pods of young peas. How sweet they were, and with the membrane peeled off their insides, even the pods tasted good. So we had peas proper one day, and topped and tailed, membrane removed, cooked and mashed pods the next. Nothing was ever wasted.

We would help pick whatever fruit was in season and take a loaded handcart the 5 miles or so to Hamlin. Just on the outskirts of the town was a jam factory. The owner was always pleased to see us. I don't know if my father ever had any money for whatever he delivered, but we had glasses of lovely cold fruit juice and doorsteps of home-made bread and jam.

Where the houses along the road through the village ended, it led on to a slope, and there on the left was a forest pub. A lot of the villagers gathered there on Sunday mornings. On the left, just before this popular watering hole, was a large, colourful meadow full of wild lupins and other flowers. Outside the pub was an age-old beech tree. The landlord had utilised one of the lower branches and had hung a swing from it. This was in constant use as the older children squabbled over whose turn it was. I couldn't reach it and had to be lifted onto the seat, which happened about three times, all told.

I walked back down to the meadow and decided to pick some lupins for Mum. They were such delicate colours. Which ones to pick? Some of them stood as tall as me. Suddenly, there in a slight hollow in front of me: a big pair of brown eyes and two huge ears. The fawn didn't move. I let the lupins slip out of my arms and fell on my knees beside the little deer. It shivered despite the warm sun. I flung my arms around its neck and nuzzled into it. I started to cry and told it that I loved it and that I, too, was alone. I was so pleased that I had found another pet. I must have clung to it for a good five minutes when suddenly, amid spasmodic sobs, I heard an unfamiliar noise. I got up quickly and ran as fast as my scared legs allowed me to. My father saw me and came running towards me. I was sobbing so hard by this time that it took a while before Dad got out of me the reason why. He called me a silly girl and we went back to my new little friend. Dad grabbed two handsful of grass and rubbed the fawn's neck with it. He then explained to me that he had to rub my smell off, otherwise when its mum came back and caught my smell, she would think it was another's fawn and would leave it, and it would have starved and died. On a number of long weekend walks we often saw deer in the distance and I always hoped one of those was my 'pet'.

Further up the road from the forest lodge pub was a beech wood, on the right. Here, when it was the right time of year, we would gather beechnuts. They were hard to find and we'd have to clear dead leaves to find the nuts underneath. We each had a tin or jar in which to collect them, and when full would empty the nuts into a larger vessel, like a bucket or big tin, into which my father was gathering the little three-cornered masts. Starting again, it seemed to take forever before just the bottom of my jar was covered. This laborious task did not end there. Back home the precious findings were tipped onto the kitchen table and the outer shells of the masts were removed, and then the nuts were minced. The little bit of oil was used for cooking, and the minced mash turned into cakes.

Past the beech wood at the top of the hill was a clearing backed by another pine wood. In the middle of this area was a big crater, quite deep, too. It had filled, over some time, with rain water. This was a great meeting place and the crater was our local outdoor swimming pool. There was panic one Sunday while everybody was out enjoying themselves, being together with their families, playing, having picnics, diving and swimming. My father had dived in and nearly didn't come up again. He was helped by several people. The general happy atmosphere was subdued and the magic of the day had gone. (I found out some years later that through diving into the water, something had affected his ears and he would have drowned had it not been for his rescuers.)

Everybody worked hard all week, but Sundays were always family days. On another Sunday walk we were approaching the edge of a forest. Suddenly, a few agitated birds were making a right racket. My father pointed out a jay in one tree and a magpie nearby as the culprits of disturbing the Sunday morning peace. Dad explained that both birds were the 'police force' of the forest, and let all the other birds and wildlife know that someone was approaching.

On another outing, I had wandered off the beaten track somewhat. I had spotted a little thing with black and yellow stripes and wanted to see what it was. Fat chance! My father happened to look to the side, surveyed the situation, and yelled for me to run to my mother. He ran off in another direction, chased by a wild boar. Dad caught up with us, still somewhat breathless, and gave a direct order aimed at me: 'Stay on the path!' That big, black and yellow 'bumble-bee', on four legs I had half-seen in the grass had been a wild boar piglet. It, like me, had been an adventurer.

I used to love the weekends and our outings. One Sunday, Dad had managed to borrow a bike for my mother and one each for my sisters and himself. We had gone further afield. I sat astride the bar of my father's bike on a cushion which had been tied around it, serving as my saddle. It did move about a bit and I had to hold on really tightly to the handlebars. We stopped for a picnic somewhere and played among wild flowers, ferns and saplings. On our way home, along a narrow mountain stream, no wider than a beck, my father stopped suddenly. Unceremoniously I was unsaddled, and then Dad was lying on his stomach alongside the stream. He waited. He waited, and whoosh! Up came his hands, in which he clenched a wriggling eel. I remember we had eel fried in butter that evening. The girls and I had a taste each. I cannot remember what it tasted like and I've never had eel since. It also escapes my memory what else was on the menu that night, except that we had the wild strawberries we had picked, with milk and sugar.

I bear the scar to this day of another Sunday walk. We had left the village behind and were walking towards a forest, along a path which ran through a farmyard. The yard was full of chickens which were all very friendly. As usual, I was lagging behind, off the beaten track and all that. I was intrigued by these chickens. They even allowed me to stroke them. By this time my family was near the stile ready to cross into a meadow. There were four white chickens which had no feathers on their necks. I called out to Dad to make him aware of this unusual feature. He laughed and assured me that they had had a shave that morning. 'Oh!' Satisfied with dad's explanation I stood up. Just then a very cross cockerel, squawking loudly and wings beating frantically, headed towards me. The darned flying thing was bigger than me! He embedded his beak in the top of my left thigh, still crowing loudly and wings flapping. It took all of my strength to stay upright. The usual happened: I screamed! Dad and the farmer arrived at the same time. I was comforted by one and the cockerel was unhooked out of my thigh by the other. Blood was pouring down my leg. The chickens had scarpered. My mother and sisters were there looking almost as though they felt sorry for me.

The farmer's wife came out with warm water, cotton wool and a big plaster (bigger than actually needed, but it looked impressive). After some welcome refreshments of coffee for the adults, glasses of cold milk and slabs of homemade cakes, and profuse thank you's, we went our merry way.

Once the corn and wheat had been reaped the school children had a harvest holiday. We would walk carefully in our bare feet, between rows of stubble, each of us with a bag of tiny deep purple pellets, dropping what we could hold between thumb, forefinger and middle finger, down each mouse hole. Along the way we could gather up any stray stalks of corn or wheat and take them home. Between three of us we used to collect quite sizeable sheaves. They were put to good use: the grain was turned to food, any which escaped the chickens would eagerly peck up, and the straw was cut up and used as bedding for the rabbits. Nothing was ever wasted.

Between the road and our house was a fenced-in orchard which belonged to the farm next door. We were all playing outside. The older ones started to throw sticks and stones up into the trees, trying to dislodge some fruit from the trees nearest this side of the fence. Then, somebody noticed a small gap at the bottom of it. With a yank here and a pull there the hole was marginally enlarged, big enough for me to be pushed through. I dutifully passed fruit through the hole in the fence, fruit which I had picked off the ground in the grass. Suddenly, I found myself on my own, staring at a pair of big black shoes. The farmer, looking quite stern, helped me out of my mesh cage. I babbled on about my mum making apple cakes and soup of pears and potatoes, just as he disappeared back to his farm.

My middle sister arrived to see how I was. How was I? Furious! Absolutely beside myself, having been left, yet again, to carry the can. I lunged at her, screaming, crying, hitting and kicking. Dad, bless him, always there when you needed him, turned up from absolutely nowhere. He separated my sister from my clasp and frenzied attack, and he gave me one hell of a hiding. It was for kicking my sister. It needn't have been her, it could have been anybody. There were three things he would not tolerate: kicking, spitting and throwing stones at a person.

The next day there was a knock on the open door. It was the farmer. I froze. He had a bucket full of apples, vegetables and a couple of jars of preserved fruit. 'For your mother, to make apple cake.' I think I managed to say 'Thank you' as he set down the bucket just inside the door.

Not long after we had moved into the house, I had met the farmer, as it had been my job to collect the milk from him in the mornings. I had been scared stiff of him. Half of his left arm was missing, and replaced by a piece of wood with a hook on the end of it where his hand should have been.

After the orchard incident our relationship became far less strained, and once I had shaken his hook I began to feel much more at ease with him. His wife always had little treats for me, and I loved spending time in their company. In a way, I became the child they never had. She would sometimes go and ask my mother if it was all right for me to have lunch or tea with them as a thank-you because I had been very helpful. Yes, by all means. No problem. (One less mouth to feed.) When I got back, I got it in the neck! 'You can help over there but you don't lift a finger here!' I was five and a half years old, for goodness' sake!

I used to walk down to 'our' farm from time to time to say hello. I'd reacquaint myself with the animals, the farmers and the hands. It was, sort of, my second home, as was the farm next door, as was Peter's place next door the other way.

My grandmother came to visit. There was great excitement prior to her arrival which, because I had been elsewhere, I had missed. When I got home and saw her in the kitchen I was so thrilled, and clasped my arms about her knees and promptly asked, 'When

17

are you going home?' Meaning, 'How long are you staying?' I knew what I was saying, I knew what I meant. I think that she did, too. But, I ended up with a clip around the ear and my bottom slapped for my rudeness. My mother was all heart.

'Oma' and I were a pair. I felt close to her. I showed her around our place and introduced her to all our animals. Peter joined in too, and between us I think that we convinced her that there was life outside towns and cities.

A professional photographer visited the village and many families had their photos taken, including us. (The very photo is hanging on my wall today; Mum and Dad had had a row about grandmother, us three having been made to wear silly ribbons in our hair, five of us looking like thunder!)

I started school that Easter. I looked happy in my photo, with my hair curled, sporting one of Mum's knitted ensembles and holding an upside-down dunce's hat, filled with goodies. Our school was a one-room affair. There were four rows of desks and benches. Each row was designated to a particular age group. School began at the age of six and finished at age 14.

Because I had had older sisters and had looked over their shoulders when they did their homework, I had been more than ready for school. I could count and add and write letters on my slate. I actually started school at five and a half. The school years started and ended at Easter time.

Peter used to come to school with me on some occasions. Otherwise he would have been at home alone, and with no one to play with. He benefited greatly, because a year later, when he started school officially, he was already part of the furniture.

School was from 8 am to 1 pm and we had the afternoon to play with and look after the rabbits and chickens, and go exploring.

The houses across the other side of the road had wire fences marking the end of their boundaries.

All sorts of edibles grew behind them: gooseberries, raspberries, strawberries, rhubarb. These fences were no barrier against our little hands and arms. One day we managed to pull a whole stick of rhubarb through the fence, leaving the big leaf stuck to the inside. We tucked into the juicy pink stick, which took us a good hour to demolish. We had the runs for a whole week!

Another time, I remember, we walked to the end of the road leading out of the village. If you turned left it led to another village, right was the turning for Hamlin. In front of us, the cenotaph. Behind this were several big fields; directly behind it a field of sugar beet. We strolled along two rows for a short distance, sat down in the cool soil and pulled out a couple of baby beets and gnawed our little teeth into the sweet flesh, soil and all.

My father had acquired a bike from somewhere. Anyway, it was his now. It was on this contraption that I learned to ride. My dad held on to the saddle, running alongside me, with encouraging words and eventually let go. I found my balance and I was off!

All too soon, my new-found freedom was taken away. Dad spent more and more time travelling further afield on his bike, seeking work. I was now the 'man of the house'. It was below my mother to 'muck' out any animals and my sisters were always too busy. And if you believe that, you are as gullible as I was at that time.

Father had been away for a while. He had secured a job as a miner and had found accommodation in a sort of B&B. He had written letters to my mother, and soon after came home one weekend to pack some more of his clothes and set off again, this time with my older sister in tow, who under his supervision ended up working at the B&B. Another photo was taken of my mother, grandmother and older sister – a sort of confirmation keepsake as she had turned 14.

After a short while my dad was employed by another mine. Houses had been built for the miners. One of these, close to the mine, a school and two local shops and tram stops, was to become ours.

I cannot remember the actual move. I do remember it being a traumatic time for me, having had to say good bye to all our animals and my pets and friends. It was one of the biggest wrenches of my young life. I don't recall what happened to our chickens and rabbits.

We were on the third floor, top right, with storage space in the attic, a coal bunker and a vegetable store in the cellar. Each one an individual lock-up space. There was a wash-kitchen in the bowels of the house, its use allocated to each flat owner once every six weeks. No dogs or cats or pets were allowed. Downstairs, below us, they had a big bird in a cage. The bird was much bigger than some of our chickens had been. If this was not a pet, what was it?

My middle sister and I were enrolled in the local school which we could see from our kitchen/lounge window. My big sister became nanny to a little farmer's boy. The following summer holidays I spent on the farm. I was in my element, surrounded by cows, chickens, pigs, sheep, goats, horses and dogs. What a wonderful holiday this promised to be. I stayed out of the milking parlour, but I helped where and when I could and did as I was told.

One morning I was given a pail of slops to feed the pigs. I pulled back the bolt on the gate and walked through it. Immediately on entry I was nudged and nuzzled and completely surrounded by squealing pigs, eager to get at the food. I just managed to empty the bucket into the trough before I lost my balance and fell head first into the stinking mud. I was covered in it, and my pride was hurt yet again. While my sister stripped me and hosed me down, she told me that I should have emptied the bucket from the outside. Thanks for the belated advice!

The village was huge compared to what I had known. Preparations for the annual summer fair were well under way. My sister had gone to the hairdresser's, and even there all the ladies had been given crepe paper of different colours and were churning out buds and flowers to embellish arches, hats and garlands galore.

My early morning acquaintance with the pigs' mess had done me no favours. My sister had pulled a dress out of the ironing basket for me to wear. I stood alongside the road and cheered the passing floats, as did the people on the opposite side. Suddenly, in a gap between floats, I spotted my parents. I waved and called. My sister saw them too, and as we went up to them she had a smack across the face from Mother, who had been totally humiliated by my dishevelled, unkempt state, wearing a creased dress! She could have ignored me and walked off. Instead I was unceremoniously dragged away, back home. My clothes and bits and bobs, and my sister, followed a few days later.

My sister went to work in a flower shop for three days a week and attended college twice a week, to study floristry.

My middle sister, by now, had left school as well and had a job with a tailoress, and later in a knitting factory. She was able to purchase cheap wool and still had staff discounts. From time to time she brought home skeins of wool which my mother put to good use.

My class and every class of every school in the district were invited to attend a gymkhana and a dog handling show in a local stadium. A competition for the best essay was announced. I had written reams on what time I got up, dressed, breakfasted, etcetera. I gave my piece to my mother to read. She crossed out most of what I had painstakingly written, saying that nobody wanted to read about my morning ablutions or my breakfast habits. Point taken!

Some weeks later our headmaster walked into our classroom. A respectful hush fell on his entry and we all stood to greet him. He didn't beat about the bush, and right away explained the rudiments of writing. He drew a straight line on the blackboard. 'That,' he said, 'is your foundation, the base of your house, the beginning of your story.' Then he drew the main part of the house. 'Your living area is the guts of your story. And this,' as he added the roof, 'is the end of your story.'

He announced the results of the competition. I had won first

21

prize! Of course, he and the whole school were very proud of my distinguished achievement. The prize was a radio. Second prize was to go to a young girl in an orphanage in a village close by – and wouldn't it be lovely for that little girl to have a radio all of her own. Wouldn't I like to...? Well, when put like that, with the eyes of my teacher, the headmaster and every pupil in the class upon me, waiting for my response, what choice did I have? I proudly went home with the second prize – a 5 mark note. I told my mother about my win and showed her the note, never to be seen again! Money was scarce, but that...! It was like taking sweets off a baby.

I had several encounters with the bird downstairs. It always seemed quite friendly. One day, it had obviously got out of bed on the wrong side of its cage, or had a bad feathers day or something. It squawked and flapped its wings, turned its back on me, lifted its tail and took aim. Thanks a lot! Covered in it, yet again!

The girl downstairs was a year older and a head taller than me. We and some other girls used to meet up and play. One of them had us all spellbound with stories of an old witch who lived in the woods. We ventured there, listening to stories about the wicked woman.

We got quite close before we were told to crouch down out of sight and keep quiet. An old woman appeared. A couple of the girls cried out and then they all ran off. Still crouched low, I watched her every move. I was fascinated. And she had animals!

I went back several times on my own, to watch her gardening or just sitting on a bench, or looked on as chickens pecked food out of her hand. Many, many years later, in another country, I thought of her again, as I had often done. I put pen to paper and wrote the following:

The Old Woman with White Hair and Wrinkled Brow*

There's a tatty timber shack down in the woods.
The one time much trodden, winding, weedy path
Has long not felt foot upon its springy moss.
This track, which was once in use, abruptly stops
Where it meets a perimeter of barbed fence.
Within the rusty, worn, wire enclosure
Is a compound, quite like a paradise.
Root vegetables and those which need staking
And seedlings, breaking through the black sifted soil,
In neat, narrow rows, side by side are growing.
Each plant looks healthier than ever I've seen.
Everything appears carefully tended.
The absence of weeds suggests love for the land.
Colourful flowers and variegated shrubs
Grow, around the base of three sides of the hut –
The fourth, which the sun hardly ever reaches
Is half covered with a slanting wood structure
Under which sawn logs are stacked against a wall.
Aside this are sheds, pens and a fodder barn
And the fence stretches between a score of stakes
Ending, where it reaches the banks of a brook,
Where the stream runs deep, the far bank rising high.
The lush grass providing plenty of nourishment
For the cow, which has recently borne two calves.
And the goat, with kid, is busily munching
At the long and fresh, succulent blades of grass.
Bright yellow chicks, a rooster and some brown hens
Strutting, scratching, among the soil and pecking.
On a line, a black and white hide of a cow
Hangs, the sun fails to rekindle it with life.
Alongside this, once investment of a cow,

---

*From *The Complete Works of My Kind of Poetry* by Gisela D. Pilot.

Bunches of aromatic herbs are drying,
Their sweet smell wafting to my place of hiding,
Behind this, larger, of the age-old oak trees.
Many a time have I stood here, to observe
This hidden sanctuary, far from beaten tracks.
On more than one occasion have I seen her:
The old woman with white hair and wrinkled brow.
As if through telepathy, she now emerges
Through the door, from within her inner sanctum.
With slow, deliberate steps she makes her way
To the gate – slightly crooked in its hinges –
Checking it, testing, if it is safely fast.
Among the narrow, earthen paths she moves now.
Stooping here and there, eliminating weeds
Which, time and again try their best to sprout up.
On her shoulder sits a broken-winged starling,
Now she bends low and pulls a worm from the soil
And offers it, on her right palm, to the bird
Which hastily squeaks its appreciation.
On the canopy, covering the chopped wood
She gently sets down her colourful patient
And continues to check over land and stock.
The bottom of her apron, made of sacking,
Is turned up to create a large-sized pocket.
From it she now extracts a handful of hay
And proffers the contents of her outstretched hand
To the cow, swiftly wandering towards its snack.
The cockerel crows, gathering his family;
The snow-white goat, quickly follows the two calves.
The woman is surrounded by animals.
She feeds a little something to each in turn
And pats and strokes them as she hands them their treats.
About two dozen birds, as though they've been summoned
Have just flown into the garden from the woods.
Eagerly pecking up any crumbs they find

24

Which the woman has shaken out of her pouch.
Slowly she walks to the far side of her home –
This side I cannot see from where I am crouching.
I move, very stealthily, softly treading
Till I'm in line and have the woman in view.
She is sitting on a bench under a tree
Which, soon, promises a splendid crop of fruit.
Drawn, as though by some unseen magnetism
The livestock, one and all, have followed her there
But, none have stepped past her, the bench or the tree –
Bar a few birds, their throats filled with evetide songs.
Slowly, she now rises and in so doing
Reveals to me a wooden cross behind her.
She stands, looking at the simple crucifix
And now, lowering herself onto her knees,
Folding her hardened, earth-ingrained hands in prayer –
Her head is bowed. I can see her face no more.
The menagerie is still. The scene serene.
I wonder who or what, rests beneath that tree
As if caring for it and feeding its roots.
As though giving it life and swelling its fruit.
Twice I have spied upon this ceremony,
This so moving and very heart-rending display.
This time, as then I, too, feel compelled to kneel
And offer upwards a prayer through misted eyes.
I rose, when she did and stumbled blindly
And clung tightly to her as I sobbed and cried.
To this day I cannot explain my action
Or say why I had not, like others had done,
Run away from that place, too frightened of her.
I remember well, the summer of that year
When I spent many afternoons with her.
She could see quite clearly with her warm brown eyes.
Not one noise would escape her acute hearing
But, due to whatever, her voice was no more.

25

I had wanted to ask her so many things.
My then so young mind of less than eleven years old.
I helped her with sharing out food for her pets.
Together we raked, hoed and tilled the rich soil
And shared some repasts when all the work was done
And sat on that bench, before I had to go.
Because she could not, I did not speak either.
Our eyes would meet or our hands would touch.
Both of us knowing what the other one thought –
Achieving far more depth and sincerity
Than a lifetime of spoken words could have done.
Short-lived were those summer days, so long ago.
Before fate moved me on, many miles away.
I have often thought about my dear old friend –
Had anybody visited her since then?
Does she still live, aft' a score and quarter years –
The old woman, with white hair and wrinkled brow?

My father came home from work one day to announce that he was going overseas for a while, to work. I cried buckets. My dad was everything to me. He was my friend. He always knew how to explain things. I relied on him. Hadn't he been the one person who had taught me so much about nature and animals? Had he not always been there when I had needed answers?

My sisters had left home by now, which meant that I would be on my own with my mother. She certainly had never been one for explaining anything. Making something out of nothing was her forte but, explaining? No.

My dad left for Wales during Easter week in 1954. After at least two letters a week to my mother, extolling all the wonderful virtues of everything green and lush that spells Wales. mother was persuaded to join him for a six-week holiday which coincided with their anniversary at the beginning of June, their twentieth.

Hurried arrangements were made to farm me out to friends of the family – I hardly knew them. They had a little boy and I was often left in charge of him while they went bowling and meeting up with their friends. In fairness, the man's parents lived downstairs. I was fetching and carrying for them, too: coal and logs, firewood from the cellar, and shopping.

School was a good 4 miles away now and I cycled there and back. On the way back I would often stop to admire some birds or insects or whatever caught my eye. This sometimes made me late and landed me in hot water. Grounded! More chores! I was all of eleven and a half by this time.

Other than a rat and mice in the cellar and upstairs, my only encounter while in the garden was with a bee or wasp or one of those nasty flying, stinging things which stung me on my left knee. It was already infected due to a fall and said 'stinger' found the very spot. My knee blew up like a balloon. I had a temperature hot enough to heat the whole of upstairs and ended up in hospital for two weeks. I was getting letters from my parents and I was writing back, but was not allowed to mention hospitals or mishaps or anything unpleasant for fear it would worry them.

Mother's six-week holiday was extended, again and again. Finally, after six months she came back, tied up some loose ends, and took me shopping: new coat, earrings, knee-length white socks, shoes, dress – Christmases, birthdays, Easter, Whitsun all rolled into one, or what? Thus, all dolled up, I arrived in Wales, in December 1954, about a week before Christmas.

Our first landlady had a budgie and a cat: what a combination. Cats are not my favourite animals, and after my last encounter with a bird, I steered well clear of the little sod.

We moved on from there and ended up in 'Mummy Powell's (as my mother had christened her) with her two daughters, a canary, a retired old, overfed greyhound and a little pooch. The latter took to my mother. It became her lapdog and followed her everywhere. She now had two admirers. It and her black hen from years ago.

We moved. I don't know how many times. One of our landladies had massive spiders in the outside toilet which at night would usually house one of the neighbours' cats too. Dozens of cockroaches, hiding in the dark under the high-backed settle in the stone-flagged kitchen, completed the menagerie.

Whenever I needed to 'go', I was on my own. I hated having to walk across the big yard. One night, a lighted candle had blown out just as I opened the door with its heart-shaped window. I sat down quickly in sheer desperation, door wide open. With that, a cat which had been sitting on top of the overhead cistern flopped onto my back. It was hard to say who was more scared!

When my mother felt the need to visit 'the place', she always insisted that I go with her, even if I didn't need to. But I might want to, once I got there! This was probably my first introduction to autosuggestion.

There was a lane across the road leading down to a brick work. Laden lorries chugged past and empty ones came back, all day. To the right of the lane was a marshy field. At the far end of it was a copse, and a stand of trees under which was a big patch of bluebells. Our Scripture teacher had expressed her fondness of bluebells. I decided to make my way across the soggy ground to pick some flowers to take to school the next morning.

I kept that gorgeous carpet of blue in my sights all the time. Halfway across I felt what I assumed to be a lump of grassy mud, land in the back of one of my quite new wellingtons. I squelched on but soon decided to remove the clod. Only it wasn't! It was a frog which, by this time, was well and truly squashed almost beyond recognition. I did the usual, and screamed! I pulled off my wellies and never wore them again, despite the fact that my dad scrubbed and bleached the one boot a number of times.

We had had quite a lot of rain, for which purpose the wellies had been bought in the first place. I had worn them once or twice before when we lodged in a previous place. A Co-op store was about half a mile away, a big meadow alongside the road ending at the shop. Behind this was a shallow stream full of stones and shiny pebbles and the clouds swam along in it. This was the way I'd walk back from the shop. Not exactly a short cut, but I was in my element, off the beaten track as usual.

The rain was followed by a long spell of dry weather which did not necessitate the wearing of protective, watertight footwear. By the autumn and the onset of wet weather again, my green, shiny wellies no longer fitted me. Thank you, up there! Whosoever had been on my side – thank you!

Easter 1956 saw my parents travelling to Germany to fetch my middle sister and her one-year-old son, whose father had been killed in a motorbike accident. Once again I was farmed out, this time to the village pub, just down the road. The owners had a young son and a little daughter and I helped to look after them.

The little boy often played on his own in the garden. There were a few chickens scratching about and the boy was sometimes asked to find worms for them. One day he rushed in and said that he had found six. Not quite believing him he took me by the hand and led me to them. He had, in fact, found one long worm and had made five cuts through it. He seemed to take a fiendish delight in watching the wriggling, writhing bits. I gathered them up and threw them to the hens. Then I marched the little murderer in for his tea.

One day I helped the landlady with some baking. She was cutting out rabbit-shaped biscuits and had measured butter and sugar into a bowl for me to mix. The butter was quite hard and already I was beginning to hate this job, and said that 'this won't come at all' just as the phone rang. The phone was always ringing. As she went to answer it she called back, 'Use some elbow grease!'

About 20 minutes later she came back to the kitchen to find the contents of the food cupboard and fridge on the floor about me. 'What the...?' I quickly, apologetically said, 'I think you must have run out. I can't find any.' Come to think of it, I couldn't remember ever having seen any elbow grease in the shops, either. There was an extra buzz in the pub that night when everybody heard of the saga of my lost elbow grease.

A couple of mornings later we were upstairs, stripping a bed, when the doorbell chimed. 'Be a love and go down for me, it will be L. He calls in every morning for his fags and matches.' It was L. I served him and he left. I ran back up, two steps at a time, beaming from ear to ear, happy to prove the landlady wrong, just this once. She was always right – about everything! Still breathless I spluttered out that yes, it had been L, and yes, he had matches – but hadn't wanted fags. 'He had twenty Woodbines instead.' How was I to know that they were fags? More laughter at my inexperienced expense in the bar that night.

Back home our landlady had a stroke and died shortly afterwards. She was in her early nineties. Although she had often told us that we could live in her house as long as we wanted, her niece and two nephews, who lived in a house at the end of the long garden, were having none of it. A verbal promise was worth nothing. Even a solicitor couldn't help us. So, it was a case of all move, including another paying tenant who had occupied one of the two front rooms. She moved up the hill to her daughter's farm. We moved even further up the mountain to a bungalow.

Dad had been to do a job for the one-time cleaner of our previous landlady. He came home with a nanny goat and two kids. Mum, Maggie, bleated her way all the way up the hill with little Jack and Lucy in hot pursuit, stopping a number of times to suckle and be close to their mum. Dad carried both kids more than they walked.

Easter was coming. There was talk of kid roast! Despite my pleas and objections I came home from school to find Jack's skinless, gutted body hanging upside down by his back legs, still bleeding. I had played with him and his sister, in the field, just the day before.

My sister had a live-in job with a couple of school teachers and their two sons. She cleaned, cooked, washed, ironed and mended. The house pet, a cat, had had kittens and my sister arrived with one of those little ones as an Easter present for my mother. What had she been thinking of? There was one person, I knew, who disliked cats even more than I did!

The kitten had a gorgeous face and lovely bright eyes. He had mainly black fur but sported four white socks and a bib. Peter, as I had named him, was not allowed indoors when my mother was about. His bit of comfort was for a couple of hours, early in the mornings when Dad came home from night shift and Peter would quickly follow him in and settle in front of the cast iron stove with an extra saucer of milk and some titbits.

I felt that Peter and I were treated pretty much the same by my mother. We always seemed to be in her way, so it didn't take me too long to warm to him and stroke and cuddle him whenever I could. This felt quite therapeutic for me, and Peter would always purr his contentment.

Dad was a great one for coming home with waifs and strays. Toffee a dog of that colour, was next to join our 'happy family'. She came from a farm, apparently having got too old, slow and fat. Then we missed seeing her around for a couple of days.

Following little noises, we found her. She had crawled through a small gap in a hedge and lay there, gasping and thirsty, having whelped five gorgeous puppies, all firmly attached to her teats.

I had to go to school. I told my friends all about the latest incident and they all wanted a puppy. I eagerly told Dad that I had found homes for all the little ones, but he told me that they had gone back to the farm. The next day, in school, I told the girls that the puppies were no longer available because... One of them asked the age of the pups and went on and on about having to be at least six weeks before they could be taken from their mother. There is always one smart Alec, isn't there! But, my dad had said that they had gone back to the farm. That was quite good enough for me, thank you. Toffee's teats shrunk in time but she always looked so sad. She and I had a cuddle and a cry for many a day.

Where we lived was a half-hour walk to the bus stop for me. From there, I took a bus into town and another one up the hill to my school. I was coming home one day and heard frantic bleating from quite a way off. I rushed home. The bungalow stood on its own. Next to it, on the left, was the free-standing garage. Adjacent to this was the field in which Maggie was staked on a long chain. Her collar and head were entwined in brambles. I dropped my school bag and crawled through the fence. Maggie was crying out for help, her eyes like organ stops.

The more she had tried to free herself the more she had got entangled. I put my arms about her neck (been there, done that before) and tried at first to calm her. I cried with her, pleading with her to please not die. Slowly, meticulously, bathed in perspiration, I released her from the captive, thorny, branches. I restaked her chain and got some water for her. I dipped my hands in it too, and stroked her face and head.

At last, I went indoors. I stood bleeding and in tatters as I greeted my mother. I had not realised that my clothes were in shreds. What time did I call this? Where had I been 'til now?

Lucy was sold to a farm down the road. Time and again Maggie freed herself, somehow, and ran all over the field trying to get to her daughter. Time and again she would lead me a merry dance before I eventually managed to stake her again.

Dad had taught me how to milk Maggie. This had become my early morning job. Part of my breakfast was a bowl of still-warm milk, which had a beautiful blue shimmer over the top. After the brambles incident, Maggie and I became good friends and she would pay heed to my 'come here' or 'stand still'.

Peter was often found sitting on the milk stand at the T-junction. The milk lorry turned up each day to collect the chums. The driver invariably had a bit of fish or some gourmet morsel for what he assumed was a stray cat.

It was October. I came home from school on Friday in daylight. The clocks went back on Saturday. Two days later I walked home in the dark. The lane was narrow and winding in parts, with high hedges either side of the last drag up the hill. At the top of this on the right was a smallholding. The lane opposite led to another farm, where my friend Margaret lived. On several occasions the farmer living on his own on his little spread took great delight in jumping out from nowhere, shouting 'Boo!'

I hated that junction with a vengeance. Quite often, Margaret became quite hysterical and wouldn't move another inch, unless I sent her. Having walked her the quarter of a mile or so down to her farm, her mum would insist on a cup of tea and something to eat, for my troubles. At home, of course, I got it in the neck again.

I hadn't been too bad in the dark before Margaret came into my life. From the bus stop, the first sign of civilisation was Margaret's aunt's place, our first pit stop, before going on our way. Margaret was a real drama queen. Every now and then, as we walked and talked our way home, she would suddenly stop, clutching her heart, frightening the daylights out of me. 'Oh my God, what's that?' or 'I can hear something.' Then again, 'Stop!' (hand clutching her heart region). 'There's a man over there.' The man was a cow's head looking out over a fence.

Just past that fence was a small opening in a hedge on the left which led uphill, across often muddy fields to her farm. We used this short-cut more and more. Me arriving home on a tractor became a regular occurrence, and I quite often had the silent treatment because I had been late, yet again.

The first day home from school after the clocks went back, I was on my own. Down in the dip I crossed a small bridge – not before I had checked all four sides for anyone lurking there. That was Margaret's doing. There was a thick fog. No street lights. No stars. No moon. I found the middle of the road, which consisted of a long line of chippings piled there by tractor, lorry and car wheels. I walked astride this guideline until I suddenly bumped into something. I was scared witless and screamed. It was one of the locals who then, sympathetically, walked me home.

The next night as I whistled my way up the last of the hill, I saw the reflection of two eyes in the middle of my dreaded junction. It was Peter. I had never been more glad of anything or anyone. He meowed his hello and I answered in my way. He kept slinking in front of my feet. I could make no headway. Finally, I picked him up, cuddled him, so glad of his company. This occurred every evening.

The weather changed. It got cold and colder. Peter slept in the coal shed. He would spend hours and hours – all day, in fact – licking and cleaning himself, and just as he started to look his pristine self again, it was bedtime once more.

Then came the snow! The lanes were cleared for the milk lorries. Mother left for town one morning and I opened the door to let Peter into the kitchen and the warm. No more spending all day licking and cleaning, help was at hand! I filled the sink with warm water and soaped Peter, ridding him of all the coal dust. We squatted in front of the warmth of the stove. I was rubbing Peter dry in a hand towel when he pricked his ears and I too heard a noise. My mother had forgotten some letters she wanted to post, and finding Peter and me, yelled in no uncertain terms 'Get out'. We did. Me clad in socks, slippers, short skirt and top and cardigan, which I took off and wrapped around Peter, who was still damp after his bath, to stop him getting cold. We walked a little way down the lane and then I shivered and sobbed my way back home after I heard the car taking off once more.

Dad, with a friend, used to go shooting in the early hours. Over breakfast he related, enthusiastically, having seen a hare family at play. I too wanted to witness this. At some unearthly hour one morning, I was awakened. If I wanted to come, I had to get up now! I was kitted out with jumpers, warm clothing and a spare pair of Dad's wellies, stuffed with screwed-up paper, and I wore several pairs of socks. The feet fitted fine. The tops of the boots, however, hit my shins and calves with every step.

We reached our destination. I was picked up onto a branch which, I straddled. I rested my head on one of my arms just as Dad whispered to me to stay alert. 'Any minute now.'

Just then a pair of long ears appeared out of a depression in the grass. The ears were followed by a whole body, nostrils flaring, testing the early morning air. Another hare appeared, gradually followed by nosy little ones. They romped and played amongst themselves. One went off to explore further afield. His dad called. There was no response at first. When there was, eventually, dad whacked his ears about his offspring and hurled him several feet away. Subdued, the youngster returned, to be welcomed back and licked by his dad. I witnessed all this from the perch in my tree. Better even than television, but maybe not as comfortable.

In school the following week I had an unexpected outing: dog walking. We had a poetry lesson, reading: 'The West Wind', by W. Wordsworth. I was still having problems pronouncing W's. I didn't realise this until I was made aware of it. The class was supposed to read the poem together. We hadn't even got to the end of the first verse when we were told to start again. This went on four or five times, and with each: 'And again!' the teacher got more and more agitated. She then picked out several girls to read the first verse in turn. My stomach was in knots and I knew she was going to ask me too. I stood up and began to recite. Between the title, the name of the author and the first line, there were nine W's! She had heard enough. 'I knew it! I don't know what you are doing in the A stream,' she yelled. 'Go to the Head at once and report to her!'

I walked dejectedly almost the full length of the corridor and gingerly knocked on the headmistress's door. On entering she beamed, 'Oh good! Be a good girl and run down to the post office and post these letters.' There were 15 of them and I needed to buy stamps for them. Almost as an afterthought she pressed a dog lead in my hand. 'And take Rusty with you, will you? He'll enjoy the walk.' On our return. Rusty was as pleased to see his mistress as she was him. I gave her the change from the money she had given me for stamps and she told me that I was a good girl.

I rushed down to the hall, quickly changed, and ran outside to join the girls of my class for netball practice. After a while there was rapid knocking against one of the window panes of the English room. The teacher was red with rage and motioned for me to come in, but the PE teacher refused to let me go. And there ended that episode. I stayed in the A stream. I was prefect, sports captain and house captain. I came top in Scripture and cookery and was sixth in English (out of 36). In the summer of 1957 all my classmates left school. Because my birthday was in late October I had to return to school for one more term.

In January 1958 I became a nanny to three young children. I was more like a big sister to them. Their father, a dentist, had a huge white horse. Silver was a bit wild and headstrong and didn't have much in the trust department. He used to scare the hell out of me. By the same token, the slightest thing would scare him, big as he was. There were two donkeys as well, and a boxer who was as wild as Silver and totally disobedient.

Silver, Coco and Neddy spent the days in the top field. There was a shelter for them for when it rained. If they weren't in it I'd sometimes walk up and whistle to entice them with some hay, apples or carrots. Once they had stood under it, in the dry, for a few minutes, they seemed to get the message.

My tactics were to work in my favour in the end. In the evenings I had to bring horse and donkeys down from the field. I chased all over it trying to catch them one by one. It was exhausting as they gave me the runaround. I am sure they thought it was playtime.

There was a huge garage, the back of which had been turned into stables. From the field down, a ranch fence had been erected all the way down to the huge tarmac area of the front and side of the property with a gate blocking off the bottom, leaving a path clear to the stables. On a couple of wet evenings I whistled and coaxed them to the shelter.

Then, on a few dry evenings, I employed my whistling tactics but stood behind the closed gate by the turn-off for the stables. I whistled half a dozen times, sounding like a snipe. It worked. The three of them came trotting down, accepted their handful of hay or apple, and happily went into the stables.

My boss had been quite impressed at how quickly I had come back in, for a couple of nights. After the third successful evening of bringing them in, I asked him to come out with me, as I wanted to show him something. My whistle had obviously become synonymous with treats. They didn't let me down! In single file they came, one behind the other, stopped at the gate, accepted my offering, turned left and walked down into the stable where fresh water, hay and a few more treats awaited them. I opened the gate, walked down the path and locked the stable door for the night. Job done. In present-day terminology, my boss was absolutely gobsmacked.

A few times, one or both of the donkeys managed to find a gap in the hedge surrounding the field and got out. We'd get urgent phone calls: 'Your donkey is in my garden', or 'is walking about on the main road'. Gawd! They gave me a hard time! I think that I had probably contributed to their escapes, because once or twice a week I would take them with me when I collected the two youngest children from the village school. The donkeys enjoyed the exercise, and the children the ride home. Once Coco and Neddy had seen what the colour of the grass was on the other side they checked to make sure of its colour a few times, before we secured all possible escape routes.

I lived in and stayed with the family for two and a half years. 'Stable girl' would have been a better handle for me. But the children became much more proficient on their bikes and I taught them to roller skate, read them lots of bedtime stories and made up lots of others, all starting with 'Once...' Yes, I believe I played my part well.

I moved back home. Peter still spent a big part of his day sitting on the milk stand, watching the world go by and waiting for his friend.

Our landlord had found a buyer for our bungalow and we moved, yet again. This time right down from the mountain, to another bungalow. Farms and smallholdings and one or two houses were dotted about, but the bungalow stood on its own. There was a stream alongside to the right of it. A field to the left was bordered by another stream, full of trout. I went fishing with Dad a couple of times. He had no time to sit on a little folding stool holding a rod and waiting for a bite. He'd send a bullet into the grassy bank, and almost instantly three or four fish would lie on the surface of the water, stunned by the noise. The victims were netted and became dinner for the day. Pigeons, roasted whole or in pies, were often on the menu too.

I sat an entrance exam for nursing and passed with flying colours. My nursing career wasn't to start for another seven months. About the same time I met my future husband. We had our first date early in March of that year.

I had a letter from my older sister, in Germany, inviting me to be present at her son's christening early in June, and to become his godmother. I didn't want to go. I was cajoled and persuaded by my parents. Then my boyfriend, too, thought that I should go. 'It'll only be for three weeks.'

My brother-in-law, a carpenter by trade, worked in the nearby mine. He had had his own business, sold it but still kept his hand in, mining by night and working with wood for a number of hours during the day. He and my sister had a two and a half-year-old daughter, and my godson was less than four months old.

On arrival I soon realised that my sister was the same as she had always been. Leopards and spots immediately sprung to mind.

They had four hutches with breeding rabbits. Chickens, ducks and a couple of geese had a fenced-in run in the long garden. A brick-built, pebbledashed building was the wash-house, which had a huge copper cauldron in it. This was fired up on wash days. I had to clean out the debris from the previous time, to light it again. I pulled out a shovelful of naked, blind baby mice while the adults scrabbled along ledges above, and in and out of coat pockets, and jackets hanging from pegs. Coming downstairs in the mornings, there'd be a black mass of scurrying mice, rushing behind the stove and kitchen cabinet.

A chicken was to be on the menu one Sunday. My sister told me to go down to the cellar with my brother-in-law, to watch him perform the deed, in case he wasn't around the next time she wanted a chicken killed – so I'd know what to do. I watched as he stunned the bird, laid it on a wooden block and chopped its head off. The beheaded chicken sprang to life, running around, still making noises and seemingly heading straight for me. I ran up those cellar steps so fast, like the very devil was behind me!

At that time, travelling out of this country required visas – for foreigners, that is. A visa was valid for four weeks. Somehow, during a conversation, this information slipped out. My sister pounced on this and took it on board. I was getting ready for my journey home. (I had been ready before the first week was out.) The morning before my intended departure I came down to find my sister on the settee in the lounge, white as a sheet and writhing in apparent pain. She looked at death's door. I couldn't leave, not with her so ill, and the two little ones. Her agony continued for another eight days. She refused doctors or hospitals. During this time I quickly wrote letters home to my boyfriend and parents explaining why I couldn't come back just yet.

The day after my visa expiry date, my sister made a miraculous recovery. She was not like a headless chook, but like a spring chicken. She went back to work the next day. I had no money left. My ticket was out of date. My visa was useless.

She had broached the subject of my staying and not going back before, because she wanted me to, and the children loved me. But I wasn't having any. No money, so 'You'd better find yourself a job!' I did. In fact I had four jobs in less than 18 months. On paydays she'd come and pick me up from work, and I would hand over my pay, for her to apparently 'save' for me. I had to beg and borrow every mark.

I was looking after the children and tending to the animals when I wasn't at work. My last job was in a carpet factory as an assistant weaver. I started in September. The daughter of an erstwhile landlady of my sister's worked there, and the company paid well. The daughter said that I had started at a good time because, just that month, a bonus scheme of 50DM a month had been introduced. I told her that I'd not see a penny of it, because...

She told her mother, who stood at the entrance of the factory the next day saying, 'Don't tell your sister about the bonus. As far as I know she doesn't know anybody here, apart from my daughter. She won't and I won't mention anything to her. Tell the office that you don't want your bonus every month, but to keep it for you.'

In December I returned from my last shift at about 10.45 to the usual scurrying of mice. A note from my darling sister said that my little nephew had fallen asleep but hadn't had his last bottle. She had been dog tired and gone to bed. My nephew, asleep in his cot, still in his day clothes and with his shoes on, woke as I let down the side of the cot. He seemed pleased to see me. I saw to him and laid him back down. For two pins I would have stayed, for him and his big brown pleading eyes. But, my plans had been made. I had to leave that night. I had made a few good friends who knew of my predicament, and knowing my devious sister, were on my side.

I arrived home at about 7 am a week or so before Christmas. Annoyed at being woken so early, my mother opened the door, glared at me, and this time it was she who asked, 'How long are you staying?'

I settled back in, got a job and evenings were spent keeping my mother company, especially when my father was on nights. We had both been reading one night. The divan during the day became my bed at night – when I eventually managed to get into it! Mother was a night owl and always reluctant to go to bed. That particular night she must have found an ounce of compassion because I had kept nodding off over my book. By the time I had made my bed, I was wide awake again. I had come to the last chapter in my book and things had really been hotting up. I waited until I thought my mother was tucked up in her bed in the room next to mine, got up, switched on the light, and before I had tiptoed back to my bed I heard, 'Put that light off, now!'

I tried again, this time smothering the switch with my pillow. A couple of minutes later my door flew open, the light was switched off and the door slammed shut again. It was no use. I'd never get to sleep, not knowing who did it. There was a torch on a shelf of an alcove. Why hadn't I thought of it before? I read the lines scanned by the torchlight. For no reason or aforethought I shone the torchlight above my head. There in the comer was the biggest spider I had ever seen!

Coming into the room from the kitchen, wooden steps on the left led up to the roof space. I moved a few pot plants and books further up, opened the curtains, grabbed my pillow and duvet, and spent what was left of the night huddled on the lower steps, keeping my eyes on the spider. I must have dozed off, when I was suddenly awoken by my dad trying to open the door, which met resistance from my feet and the bottom of the duvet. I pointed up to the creature. Dad got on the bed, reached up, grabbed the spider, took it outside, and that was that. I still don't like spiders to this day, but I am not scared of them any more.

Although letters from my boyfriend had been hidden and withheld by my sister, we met up again and resumed our courtship. I had been home for less than two months when he informed me that he was off to Africa for a few months, with his job. It was four months before he came back. Christmas Eve, that year, we got engaged, and married in September 1963. On our honeymoon in Minehead we saw a squirrel. Neither of us had ever seen one in real life and we followed it up the road, but it was too quick for us.

We lived with my husband's parents for several months before moving into our bungalow on a new estate. One of the neighbours came over one day with a beautiful collie in tow. Did I know of anybody who had lost one? She and her husband had a huge German Shepherd, fenced in, in their back garden, and couldn't keep the stray, so could I look after it, please, for the time being?

She was a darling of a dog, very placid and obviously used to family life. Within days she settled in, and as soon as I had put the children to bed, she lay in front of the closed nursery door, guarding it with her life.

My husband had been away in London, on a course. He came home for the weekend greeted by growls from the by now over-protective dog. I had to calm it, explaining that the man was a friend. As I accepted the 'stranger', so did the dog. But, my husband was not a dog person.

He had to leave again for London on Sunday night. The following weekend, having been told that my husband wouldn't be home for a couple of weeks, I saw an ad in a paper offering cheap rail fares to London. I got my in-laws to baby and dog-sit. The weekend was to be a surprise. It didn't work out the way I had envisaged. Getting back home, the news wasn't good

42

either. As my mother-in-law had opened the door to get in the milk, the dog had squeezed past her and taken off. 'I am so sorry!'

We were in our bungalow for the best part of five years before my husband's job took us to Hampshire. I enjoyed the company of one of our neighbours in particular, and her family. They had two dogs, a German Shepherd and a small 'bitsa', and we often took them for walks together.

My boys came home from school saying their little friend's dog was having puppies. Could we, please, have a puppy? I was expecting our fourth baby, and my friend tried hard to talk us out of having a pet. Three little livewire, boisterous boys, a new baby and a puppy?!

We went to see the puppy and its siblings. We all picked the same one, but it was still too young. The boy's mother said that she would keep Brandy for as long as need be, to see how things panned out with the new baby. Unfortunately he lived for only less than three days. He had spina bifida. Eventually Brandy joined our household. He was by no means a substitute for our great loss, but the boys had set their hearts on having a dog.

My friend and I were having a cuppa one morning with some biscuits. Macky, her 'bitsa' dog, sat and watched, begrudging us every mouthful. 'Do you want some?' my friend asked the dog. 'What do you say?' He promptly responded with half a yap and half a bark, with a bit of a growl thrown in.

I couldn't wait to get back over the road. Armed with a few biscuits and little treats, Brandy's education began. After 20 minutes of me doing the yapping and barking and asking, he finally got the message. After that: 'Do you want?' 'What do you say?' and 'Sit!' meant food. And by asking for it nicely, Brandy had his just rewards every time.

The boys took it in turns to take 'their' dog for a walk after school, until one day out of sheer excitement it was Brandy who was doing the taking. His walker had the good sense to let go of the lead after he had fallen and been dragged along the drive for a couple of feet. I carried him in for a cuddle and to have his knees cleaned, bathed and plastered. 'I don't like Brandy any more,' he sobbed.

The back door opened inwards, behind which, and in front of the boiler, was Brandy's box. Even when he had outgrown it and his bed was an old sleeping bag it was still called the 'box'. When I said to Brandy 'Get in your box!' he knew I meant it.

Sometime later I found a part-time job. Two days a week. I didn't think it was fair for any dog to be left on its own. I found a new home for Brandy.

Our time in Hampshire was fraught with traumas, little accidents and mishaps, but for all that we had five happy years there and even now, after 40 years, still count erstwhile neighbours as close friends.

We moved back to Wales and lived in Langland, Swansea, for two and a half years. We had a fenced-in garden with shrubs in the three borders, and other than garden birds we had no wildlife. I opened the lounge window one morning, looked out and around, and there it was! A dead rat with its throat gaping red. I shut the window, rushed through the dining room, the kitchen and out to the covered-in side, locked the two end doors, then the kitchen door behind me. I grabbed my keys, locked the front door, and somersaulted over the dividing wall and rushed next door. Although sympathetic, my dear, kind neighbour laughed over a cup of tea and assured me that dead rats don't open doors!

We moved to West Wales to a little village with its own school, post office and two garages. We had a good-sized garden with farmland behind that. From one of the back bedroom windows I witnessed my first ever birth of a calf. Another cow looked to be in difficulty, for her calf seemed to be hanging half out for ages. I phoned a farmer, who reached the cow after crossing two fields. He donned his 'midwife' hat and the miracle of another new birth lay on the grass.

The farmer's young daughter was in school with the boys and

they and I enjoyed helping with the haymaking, followed by wonderful farmhouse teas.

I picked mushrooms in the surrounding fields. I went further afield one morning and clambered over a gate with my bucket and knife. I hadn't gone very far, cut no more than half a dozen, when a herd of young heifers and steers came charging towards me. I ran back to the gate and just managed to get up and over it before they got to it too.

We ended up with a beautiful liver and white English springer spaniel. Brandy's father had been called Whiskey, his mother Ginny, so this one had to be diluted. Shandy was a lovely-natured dog and he, too, learnt to 'ask'. He didn't like the lawn mower and usually tried to help by chasing it. One day I put him on his lead while I cut the grass. The previous day he had slipped his collar and charged around the field behind, full of exuberance. I let him have his time on his own for a bit before I coaxed him back with, 'Do you want...?' while I punched another hole in his collar.

I had finished cutting the grass but not finished with clearing up. I needed something from the shop a couple of miles away. I jumped into the car and met the boys off the school bus, and drove to the shop. The boys bought what I needed and we were back home in just over half an hour. My youngest had already asked where Shandy was. He rushed around the back, no Shandy! We called. We whistled. We scoured the fields and neighbourhood. We waited. We asked around. Nothing! After a couple of weeks we gave up. His kennel and lead were where I had left them. His collar was done up. Having tightened it the previous day, there was no way he could have slipped it. That, in a way was a comfort. Somebody had obviously taken him. So, maybe he wasn't lying dead in a ditch somewhere.

Friends of ours from Genoa spend their summers down south, in Calabria. During our first holiday there I had disturbed a wasps' nest while tidying a patch of ground and got stung. Other than chirping birds, hundreds of crickets and their incessant noise, the only other thing that disturbed the peace was the morning and evening parade of cows and sheep with their gonging collars being walked out to the fields, along the path past the grounds of the house, and back again to their sheds and barns. It was a pleasant sound though, and between the 20 or so animals formed quite a little orchestra.

During our second visit, our friends had bought some little chicks. By the time we arrived they were fully feathered, quite grown up and looking quite healthy but still very young. Apart from one, a white one: its feathers looked grey and tatty. Hanna wasn't feeding or drinking. I picked her up and felt over her body – like I knew what the hell I was doing! I took her into the garage and the sink. I filled one hand with water and stuck her beak into it. No thank you, I'm not thirsty. I tried the same with food. Same response. This went on for several days. I'd pick her up and hold her in my arms and on my lap and talk to her, telling her that she must eat and drink or she'd get even more ill. She looked at me and listened, and answered by making little chicken noises. She felt quite at home on my lap. (Were men dressed in white, strait-jacket at the ready, about to come for me?) At last, on the fourth day she drank water out of my hand and even pecked a few grains. I praised her and her clucking responses got to be more chicken-like.

The next morning, as I stepped outside, Hanna was there waiting. I sat on the patio chair and waited for her to come over to be picked up for her usual cuddle. She came towards me, looked up at me, clucked and clucked, turned away, walked a few paces, came back, clucked some more, turned and walked off again.

It was like a scene from a *Lassie* film years before. I got up and followed Hanna, just as I thought that she wanted me to. Round the side of the house, shaded from the fierce summer sun and where all the other chickens were, Hanna pecked seeds out of a flat dish. Then she went and quenched her thirst from the water bowl. She walked back towards me. I picked her up and we assumed our usual position on the chair. Hanna stayed for a few minutes before she became anxious to be set free. She clucked as if to say, 'I can do this by myself now', and strutted off to join the other chickens.

Sentimental slob that I am, I had tears in my eyes. Our host laughed and said, 'I don't know why you bothered! Before we leave, they'll all have their necks wrung and end up in the freezer in Genoa.' Who knows, one of these days somebody, somewhere might even offer me a job as a 'chicken whisperer'.

We holidayed on a number of Greek islands. One of our favourite ones we visited about six or seven times, staying in the same resort. Just down the road from our accommodation was a shop with a caged parrot outside. It was one of the tattiest, scruffiest birds of its species you could have wished to meet. Every morning, we'd stop by on our way to the beach. It used to talk, by all accounts. Each day, morning and evening, I'd greet him, 'Hallo Scruffy!' As if that wasn't enough, I'd rub salt in the wound and call him a scruffy little git. Halfway through our second week, even before I got to his cage, he called out. 'Hallo Scruffy!' Cheeky little sod. Who was calling who 'scruffy' now? Two years later we returned. He remembered us. He didn't seem himself and only said Hallo. I tried to get him to add 'scruffy', but no. He looked dejected and not at all happy, let alone healthy.

That was our last holiday before we moved to Cwmbran.

Feathers, Spikes and Fur
(1985–present)

Contents

Characters

Robin	
Hoppy	Blackbird
Tatty	Magpie
Scruffy	Magpie
Sam	Squirrel
Spiky	Hedgehog
Whowho	Owl
Chaffy	Chaffinch
Nutty	Nuthatch
Starry	Starling
Miner	Starling
Bluey	Starling
Cooer	Collared dove
Bossy	Blackbird
Blacky	Blackbird
Sooty	Blackbird
Tizzy	Cat
Honey	Cat
Tiger	Cat
Ginger	Cat
Mouser	Cat
Roamer	Cat
Lurker	Cat
Pouncer	Cat
Sally	Sam's mate
Springer	Sally's offspring
Skipper	Sally's offspring
Scamper	Sally's offspring
Digger	Mole

Spotter	Thrush
Lucky	Blackbird – young
Baby	Blackbird
Podgy	Chaffinch
Shirty	Robin
Gaffer	Blackbird
Clown	Starling
DJ	Dove
Porter	Wood pigeon
Ballerina	Song thrush
Woody	Great spotted woodpecker
Chubby	Chaffinch
Tubby	Great tit
Dapper	Tit
Brucy	Tit
Minstrel	Cat
Starry	Starling
Spiky	Hedgehog
Hedgy	Hedgehog
Prickles	Hedgehog
Winger	Robin
Dovey	Cooer's mate
Sonny	Sally's boy
Skelter	Sally's boy
Sandy	Skipper's missus
Stripper	Baby squirrel
Jay	
Lucy	Chicken
Blackytu	Son of Blacky and Sooty
Wasps	
Mr Wren	
Jenny-Wren	
Bully	Hedgehog

Introduction

Since moving to my present house in 1984 I have become far more aware of wildlife. I have spent many enjoyable hours watching and getting to know the garden birds, hedgehogs and squirrels. I have written 60 stories about the garden and its wildlife, as and when anything interesting took place. The following stories cover all four seasons over many years.

No day is exactly like the previous one, nor will tomorrow be like today. Bringing my garden and its residents into your home will, I hope, enable you to enjoy it with me. It is May now as I write this Introduction, and the colours are coming to life again. One little resident has 'written' the first chapter, 'The Garden in May', and I will leave him to show you around.

The Garden in May – by Robin

My garden hasn't always been like this. It has been a garden for, I'm told, about 12 years. Other than trees having grown taller and shrubs spread wider, there had been little change. Since last summer, however, there have been lots of changes. There are new conifers, cypresses, rhododendrons, rose bushes, ground cover creepers, tulips, daffodils, snowdrops and crocuses, shrubs, herbs, heathers, azaleas, and bird boxes. The human has worked wonders since she moved here and transformed my garden into a beautiful place.

I say 'my' garden because I actually live here and share it, to some extent, with lots of others. Let me introduce myself. My name is Robin and I live here with my wife and our young family. I suppose you could call this garden and the way we live a sort of commune. We usually take our meals together, but then the rest is up to every individual couple, the young and the unattached. There are many couples, like us, who have found shelter and food here. Others come and go and pass through from time to time. I'll introduce you to some of the other characters now so that you can familiarise yourself with them.

Hoppy is a blackbird and a particularly good friend of ours, mainly because we were the first to see him after his terrible leg injury. Or, it could be due to the fact that since his accident he has been shunned by his own family. Everybody calls him Hoppy, which he doesn't seem to mind at all. Although his leg is much better now, it will never be right again and will always be deformed. He has made a remarkable recovery and an admirable job of looking after himself. Earlier this Spring, there had even been rumours of a wedding, but that seems to have fallen through. Poor Hoppy! I suppose we all look for perfection in our respective partners.

Tatty, a magpie, is a mixture of black and white and is very aptly named. She, too, like Hoppy, seems to have had a hard time of it and had been a bit of an outcast.

Scruffy, again a very suitable name for him, looks just like his name suggests. He and Tatty have been getting on quite well together lately, being of the same colouring. Between them, they do a grand job of policing the area. Well, in my opinion, anyway.

I must tell you about Sam. He is a grey squirrel and lives down in the far corner of the garden next door, high up in a tree. The bottom of that garden is wild and neglected and ideally suited for any squirrel's drey. Sam spends hours in our garden and delights us all with his squirrelly antics. Last year, the human Lady gathered all the hazelnuts from under the big hazel bush right down the far end of the garden, and took them indoors to ripen. During the cold wintry spells, and even now, she throws nuts and other titbits out. Sam has a great time looking for them, burying them and frantically digging them up again, to nibble them on the lawn or up in the great old oak, where he'll sit on his favourite branch, letting his little jaws work at double speed.

He seems to accept the fact that this oak is rather a special tree as, apparently, it yields acorns as well as hazelnuts, fir cones, peanuts, almonds and walnuts which magically appear, thanks to the Lady.

A friend of Sam's has visited the garden a couple of times but as Sam seems to regard the great tree and most of the garden as his domain, the visitor only stayed a short while. Come to think of it, it's been a long time – gosh, it must be nearly six months since the last visit. I wonder if they fell out over some nuts?

Sam doesn't like the cats either. Then, being a squirrel, he wouldn't. One or two of the cats have tried to claw their way up the thick trunk of the oak, in pursuit of Sam. Silly things, you'd have thought that any traits of their jungle cousins would have been bred out of them by now.

When Sam gets fed up with a staring contest between a cat and himself he deftly slips away, higher up into the oak, and from there along the familiar branches of the trees, growing along the stream, to where the two gardens meet and to the safety of his drey, leaving the cat to wonder where Sam is, and how to get back down the trunk.

Spiky the hedgehog and Whowho the owl we only see occasionally. But Chaffy, Nutty, Starry, Miner, Bluey, Cooer and their respective partners and families make up the rest of the bird commune. As you have gathered, we all have nicknames and with these, you will be able to identify everyone – much easier than having three John's, a couple of Ann's and so on.

Oh! This is such a beautiful place now. The new rose garden should be a spectacular sight soon. Where the rose garden ends, the rockery, with all the different heathers, begins. This used to be an eyesore of a compost heap before the Lady transformed it.

Bossy, too, is a blackbird. He gave his own kind a terrible time during the winter. I remember when the big garden was covered in snow. For weeks it remained tightly packed. Even after it had melted, the ground yielded nothing while the frost kept a firm grip on everything. Not that we expected to harvest anything in the middle of winter, anyway. But as soon as Bossy saw someone pick something up, he was there, like a shot. The nosey parker had to know what was going on and wanted to know exactly who had what. Honestly, he was worse than any taxman.

The human helped us out during the winter. She was really marvellous. Even now, when we have a plentiful supply of food, she still insists on giving us at least three square meals a day. This is a busy time for a lot of us. Sometimes we wouldn't know from where the next beakful would be coming, if it were not for the Lady. Her table is varied and certainly much appreciated. And all we can do is to repay her in kind and sing for her.

Blacky and Sooty are blackbird friends of ours too and we frequently see them and enquire after their youngsters. Animals sometimes roam around the garden, cats in particular. There is Tizzy and Honey from next door, Tiger from over the other side of the stream. Ginger, from goodness knows where, Mouser and Roamer with neither a home or a collar between them, and Lurker and Pouncer. Menaces, all of them, and a darned nuisance. I quite hate them and I don't think the human likes them much either, because they deposit their mess all over the garden.

She keeps a flowerpot with stones in, by the side patio door. They are for the cats! As soon as one of these feline creatures is sighted and, usually, Tatty, Scruffy, Blacky and Sooty are the first to spot them, they proceed to make enough racket to wake the dead. Then the Lady comes out to investigate and throws one or two stones in the general direction of the furry offender. Not aiming to hit, you understand, just to scare it off.

A couple of times, while Blacky and Sooty had popped next door and had left their babies unattended, Tizzy had tried to get at them. He could have injured them with his sharp claws, or even smothered them. Don't get me wrong. Blacky and Sooty are marvellous and not ones for neglecting their parental duties. It was just unfortunate that Tizzy had been about at the wrong time.

Opposite the roses, where a children's sandpit once was, stands an old, rusty, cement-encrusted wheelbarrow, now full of soil and planted with all sorts of bulbs and flowers. The magnolia is past its best and is beginning to drop its pale pink, waxy petals. The new conifers, rhododendrons and cypresses have taken well and have quickly adapted to their new surroundings.

Violets, buttercups, nettles, dandelions, daisies and lots of flowering weeds are allowed to grow freely along the banks of the stream. The bottom lawn is a dense carpet of bluebells and red campion. The two complement each other beautifully. The foxgloves are getting taller every day. The herb garden could do with some attention, but the wide shrub border looks delightful with all the different colourful and variegated foliage. Here too, some new flowers, shrubs and bulbs have been planted. Dainty little pansies, violets and mosses are in full bloom, heralding the summer flowers, to be followed by those which will bloom later in the autumn.

There are five new, sturdily made, nesting boxes. Three on the left fence, where the rose garden is, one on the fence behind the shrub border and the fifth hangs about 12 feet up on the trunk of the majestic oak. None of the bird boxes are, as yet, inhabited, but each one has been thoroughly inspected and investigated with much curiosity, and more than likely, earmarked for future use.

'Come on! Tea time. Come and get it!' Ah! That's the Lady calling. It will be like rush hour on market day in a minute. There is a lovely variety of food. Plenty of it, too, for everyone.

Our little ones seem to love currants. The wife and I are looking forward to the day when they'll be strong enough to leave the nest and fly onto the patio with us, so that we can show them off to the Lady of the house. After all, she'll be expecting us to bring them to tea.

I hope that you will enjoy the garden and all who live in it. Signing off now. Chirp. Chirp.

Robin

Sam

With regal majesty, the aged oak stands tall and firm on the upper lawn, dominating the garden. High above the grass it spreads its gnarled branches, boughs and twisted twigs, swelling now with brown buds. Soon the annual cycle will once again have reached completion, and the huge tree will be a vast, leafy umbrella.

A grey squirrel pays frequent visits to the garden. He convulses its small body as he buries the last of the acorns, still scattered on the grass, and is delighted when he finds other nuts which have been put out for him.

I have named the squirrel 'Sam'. He has fought with another of his kind in the past, or perhaps it was a twig or a carelessly discarded piece of wire. Whatever it was, it has closed Sam's left eye to a mere slit, surrounded by yellowy, horny skin which has grown above and below the aperture which was once a bright button of an eye.

Sam scrabbles up the thick trunk of the oak to the fork of the first bough, and with rapid jaw movements nibbles open the shell of one of last year's hazelnuts, to get at the sweet kernels. I collected all the green, fallen nuts, which have ripened in a bowl indoors. This spring they serve as treats for Sam.

When our little friend has eaten his fill, either sitting in that favourite fork of his or hunched on the lawn, with his tail elegantly erect up behind his head from where the broad, silver-streaked end curves away into an arch, he inspects his surroundings. He hops this way and that, nut in mouth, looking for a suitable burial place. He frantically digs a hole with the claws of his short front legs, and then pushes the nut into it with his nose, as far as the opening will allow. He racks his body to apply maximum strength, tail almost straight out, and arched rear end for extra effort and balance. Deftly he scratches soil and grass over the opening, pats everything down, even placing a leaf or two on top for additional camouflage, leaving the future store in its dark earthy tomb. There is many a cache in the two lawns and the borders.

A couple of magpies chatter noisily from the loftiest part of the oak's crown. They and many other birds are flying in pairs now, swooping down to the patio to feed. Three times a day I put out food for them. What pleasure I get from watching the variety of birds. Some are gathering last week's grass cuttings, which slipped through the lawn rake, twigs, moss and the like, suitable as nest building materials. Would that educated, superior man could thus conduct himself, court his love, build a home and then, and only then, bring his offspring into the world.

Sam hops across the lawn and claws a little way up the stout trunk, and with one swift move, flips his body a full 90 degrees and now looks down to the base of the oak. Like an overgrown bat, he hangs there, gripping the bark with his claws. Slowly, with deliberation, he descends again, as he has spotted another nut. Gently he threads his way through the daffodils still in full bloom, at the base of the oak. How much respect he seems to show for these Easter flowers. Back up the trunk for about 10 feet, and another quick flip, and – dear me, doesn't the lawn look odd when it changes place with the sky!

Is Sam wondering why he keeps finding hazelnuts under the oak, of all places, and at this time of year? His tail is spread flat against the wood and now he is stretching his front legs and upper body away from the tree trunk, making it look as though he is hanging out to dry. Evening comes quickly as the sun allows itself to be drawn down behind the western horizon.

Sam climbs high up in the old oak and he sits there for another moment, nibbling at a few of the new shoots. A quick scratch here and there is followed by a full stretch. Now he is pulling himself along a bough and almost wraps himself around it. Yet again an urge to scratch, and finally, expertly, running his beautiful

66

tail through his front paws and mouth, seemingly fluffing it up a little more.

He is off! Running along the lofty boughs, flying to another of the neighbouring trees, catching at a twig in passing, as it sways and bounces with the extra weight, leaping from branch to branch, from tree to tree which grow along the meandering stream. Always the same route, the same familiar scented branches, to the last tree in the farthest corner. Here, where the two gardens meet, is a drey which Sam calls home, high up, hidden from preying eyes and possible danger.

Good night, Sam!

Ambush

It was one of those rare, gloriously sunny mornings of the late spring, early summer calendars. I took my coffee and sat out on the patio. Even the soft, warm breeze was only a merest breath as it touched my face in passing. Breakfast for the birds consisted of bread, boiled rice and currants, the latter being a firm favourite with the blackbirds, robins and thrushes. These, some finches and tits, all had young to feed.

Sooty had laid five eggs in the nest she and Blacky had constructed in the honeysuckle on top of the fence, which divides my garden from next door. After Tizzy, the big grey Persian next door, had shown far too much interest in both honeysuckle and fence, I decided to investigate. That is when I found the nest with its precious eggs.

New life was brooding and the neighbours' cats were kept in as much as possible. The next time I checked the nest, the chicks had hatched. Naked, blind, exhausted, with not a feather between them, they lay in the safety of their home. The intensity of feeding grew daily, as did the chicks. Blacky and Sooty gathered the currants with much dexterity and determination. Always five in their beaks at a time. Never four. Never six. Always five.

Their approach to the nest was never a straightforward one. Cautiously, they would first settle on the fence, a tree or bush, and only after a good look around, and satisfied that there was no danger, did they go to their young. A good method which seemed to work well. About 12 days passed. I could hear Sooty and Blacky. Their startled, clattering cries and angry clucks were ear-shattering. When I went out to see what all the fuss was about. Tizzy was sitting on the fence and his younger companion, Honey, was on the lawn below, running in three directions at a time. I tried to shoo Tizzy off the fence. With sheer defiance in his livid eyes he stared at me, as if to say, 'It's our fence, I can sit here if I like.'

My neighbour, attracted by the noise of the birds, came out to take the cats indoors. Too late! The damage had been done now. The nest was empty!

Tizzy's owner had watched as the helpless chicks had fallen out of their nest and hopelessly made their getaway. Their wings, which were still only little stubs, were not yet ready for flight. They flapped about. In their panic they found the strength needed to get to safety.

Once the danger had passed, it seemed that more birds than ever were in the garden. Several, in turn, sat close to Blacky on the fence and I swear they asked him what had happened. Then they flew about almost as though a search party had been organised, to look for the premature fledglings.

I joined in the search, to no avail. Realising that my presence and good intentions could easily be misconstrued and that I was probably more of a hindrance than a help, I retreated indoors, made myself a cup of coffee and took it outside.

Even as I sat there, on the patio chair, Sooty was on the fence, almost within my reach. She kept on clucking and looking about as though she was trying to encourage her little ones back to the nest, and letting them know that it was safe again.

Then, the most extraordinary thing happened. Sooty looked straight at me and tilted her head to one side and gave out the most pathetic little peep, which seemed to ask, 'Do you know where my babies are?'

It was heartrending. I cried for her, allowing my tears to roll freely down my cheeks. I felt so inadequate. Aware of my shortcomings I went inside. There had been enough upset in the garden for one morning, without me adding to it or turning my coffee into a salty solution.

I put out more bread and currants. After quite a while, I noticed Blacky and Sooty helping themselves to the dried fruit again and flying off in different directions in the garden and the shrubs next door. I was delighted about these obvious signs of life. To celebrate this happy turn of events, I refilled my cup and sat on the patio again, enjoying the sunshine and velvety breeze which brushed my face.

Just then, I heard a rustling noise coming from the bottom of the fence. When I looked down, I saw one of the blackbird chicks trying to free itself from between a rosebush branch and the fence. At the same time, the little one tried to get through the much too narrow slats of the fence. I bent down and gently cupped one hand around the protesting nestling and pulled away the thorny stem with my free hand. Satisfied that the chick was not injured, I carried the little one across the lawn. It opened its gape as wide as a yawn and let out the loudest peep it could muster, which for all the world, sounded like 'Maaaaam'.

Blacky and Sooty heard the peep too. One in the oak, the other perched on the fence, both of their clattering cries and chattering yells piercing through the air. Were they happy or were they shouting at me?

I set number five down on the bottom lawn. It half hopped and half flapped towards the nearest tree and the cover of ivy which hugged the trunk. In a natural, inward dent of this very trunk, the little bird stayed for two days and nights. This temporary accommodation was neither safe nor suitable, as it was only a couple of feet above the ground. With the help and advice of its parents, it took up residence in the big holly bush which is the backdrop to the rockery.

Blacky and Sooty certainly had their work cut out, flying to five different sites to feed their little ones. Although the youngsters had a hard lesson forced upon them so early in their lives, at least they were still a complete family.

Sun, Rain and Diamonds

For once, the weatherman's forecast was right. Not a day ahead or behind. Not a county or two away. 'Showers, some heavy rain, with occasional sunny periods.' And it was happening just like that, right here, as predicted.

The showers were more of a deluge, really. The big globular raindrops looked as though they were all threaded on lengths of invisible string. Between the countless, slanting strings, hailstones fell heavily, bouncing as they met resistance. Then, as if by magic, an unseen puppeteer, high above, lifted the wet string curtain.

The watery, winter sun pushed a few black clouds aside and suddenly everything glistened and gleamed. The droplets of rain clung to the otherwise bare branches, boughs and shrubs. The whole garden looked as though it had been embellished with brilliant diamonds which sparkled and shone in the bright sun. A thousand gems hung on the washing line. Dozens of them dropped onto the hard flagstones below, after a blackbird took to its wings from the blue plastic line.

Pearl-like droplets of rain danced on shiny, flat leaves. When too many of them crowded the improvised small skating pads, they slid off the edge onto lower foliage or dropped to the ground. There ended the individuality, as with a final, inaudible ping, the droplets shattered and merged with those gone before them to form an overall damp and soggy puddle.

Gently, gravity tugged at each of the sparkling gems and one by one, they too fell onto the waterlogged ground where they merged into silvery puddles. Soon the twigs and branches were naked again, bereft of their jewels, silhouetted against the once more darkened sky, heavy again with thick rain clouds.

After the next downpour, the brilliant scene would be repeated, like an action replay.

The White Rain – by Springer

Skipper was raring to go out and explore the soft stuff which had turned everything white overnight. Mother pulled him back gently, but firmly.

'Not so fast, son. You don't even know what's out there,' she said.

'Oh! But mum...'

'Skipper! Don't argue,' scolded Dad. 'Just sit still and listen to your mother. You too, Springer, and you, Scamper.'

'Yes Dad,' came as from one mouth, and Skipper, Scamper and I listened attentively.

'Skipper,' Mother's voice broke the awkward silence, 'do you know what all that white is out there?'

'Ehem, it ... it looks like white rain, Mother, and I think its called em, sno...snow!'

Well! Mother and Dad were quite amazed by Skipper's knowledge. Needless to say, Scamper and I were pretty impressed as well. Our parents had put off telling us about the hard times of winter until it became absolutely necessary, like now! Apparently, we don't get a lot of snow in these parts. Skipper scratched behind his ear, looking thoughtful and quickly explained his wisdom.

'Yesterday, while I was in the big garden, I heard the magpie chatter to the pigeon about the snow.' Skipper got more and more excited as he began to relate what he had heard and who had said what, to whom.

'Well, that's what Magpie said, anyway,' he continued. 'Magpie said, "It will snow tonight. I can feel it in my beak. You mark my tail feathers – we will have snow tonight!" So, you see, Mother, Dad, I figure that Magpie's feelings in his beak must have been right and I reckon this white stuff must be what he was on about – snow – see!'

Mother slipped away and Dad sat quietly for a moment. Then just as Mum came back with food from the pantry, Dad said, looking at Skipper, 'Quite right, son.'

Dad sat very upright now and made a grunting sort of noise in the back of his throat. This was always an indication that he demanded our undivided attention.

'Yes, Skipper heard quite right. And, what Magpie said was correct, of course, I ... I, em, what I mean is, I could feel it too. Em, last night, that is, after you three had gone to bed, I said to your mother,' and turning to face Mum and pointing his right arm in no particular direction, he emphasised, 'Didn't I say to you, Sally, that I felt that there was snow in the air?'

'Yes dear,' Mother agreed.

Scamper, who was the last born of us three, was quite awestruck and shouted with glee, 'Dad, I think you are the cleverest dad in the whole area and in all the places I know.'

'Well, yes,' Father agreed casually. 'And I'll teach you all I know, just like my father taught me what he had learned from his father. Now then, eat your breakfast, your mother will want to clear up.'

'Dad, can we go out to play when we have finished, please?' I asked.

Before Dad had a chance to answer, Mum did it for him. 'No dear, not yet. Not until you know more about this wretched snow. It might look pretty, but it can be very dangerous. What do you say, Sam?'

'Yes, love, that it certainly can. Anyway, I'll leave you to explain to the children while I have a scout around. And you lot, behave and mind what your mother tells you,' he warned.

We had just settled down to what we thought would be one of Mum's long lectures of dos and don'ts, when Dad came back. He brushed himself down, shook his head and shivered.

'Goodness me! It's cold and deep out there. All the trees are thick with snow and on the ground you can barely put one foot in front of the other without ending up waist-deep in snow. Ugh! I hate the stuff!'

Mother looked worried. 'Well, that's it. I'm afraid it's going to be a day in for you three. We'll play "I spy with my little eye" and we'll listen to the birds and try to guess which song belongs to which bird, shall we?'

'Oh, but Mum,' Skipper protested, 'can't we go out for just a little while, please? Pleeeease?'

Scamper and I quickly joined in and our combined pleading, it seemed, had the desired effect. Mum and Dad talked quietly to each other. Poor Mum. She looked as concerned as ever. Then it was obvious that she and Dad had reached a compromise.

Dad patted Mum on her shoulder and reassuringly told her, 'Now don't worry, dear. They'll be all right. See you in a little while.'

They hugged each other and then Dad turned to us.

'OK, kids. Let's go. Now, you watch me closely and you only go where I go. Is that quite clear?'

We nodded eagerly, thrilled to, after all, be able to explore this new white world. Soon we had reached the big garden, step by step. Gingerly we trod, just like Dad. Talk about following in father's footsteps! We jumped and rolled about in the snow. It felt cold at first which got right through to our skin. But, with all our frolicking about, we soon got used to the snow and after a bit we even felt quite warm. We jumped and skipped about out of sheer delight, landing on the thick, soft blanket which had turned the naked branches of the trees and hedges and yesterday's green grass, white. And Dad showed us how to make snowmen. Boy, this was fun!

'Isn't this exciting, Skipper?' Only then did I realise: where was Scamper? I looked around. Here was Dad. There was Skipper. But where was Scamper?

Until that moment. Mum had anxiously listened to our frolics and she and Dad had called to each other.

'Everything all right, Sam?'

'Yes, dear,' Dad had replied.

Now the calling had stopped. A deadly hush crept over the

garden. Even the birds weren't chirping. The silence was horrible. Where Skipper and I had stopped in our tracks, looking around to see if we could spot Scamper, fresh snow fell heavily on us. And yet, it had stopped snowing everywhere else. By the time we had shaken and brushed the snow off our heads and backs and wondered why only the two of us should be snowed upon, we were covered again. We were about to call to Dad when we noticed his look of horror and dismay.

Mum's maternal instincts had told her that there was something wrong, and in a flash she was at Dad's side. Both of them looked up to the old tree directly above us. It was from one of its big branches that moments before, snow had fallen on us.

Mother motioned to us to keep quite still. We hardly dared breathe, let alone move. We both wanted to run to Mum but she looked so frightened that we just froze to the spot. Only when Dad proceeded to climb the tree did we allow our eyes to gaze up after him. We both saw Scamper at the same time. It was he who had thrown snow on us. He was the reason for our concern and fright!

Mum, in a quavering voice called after Dad, 'Oh! Be careful, dear.'

'Whoopee! Come on up, you two. This is great fun,' we heard Scamper calling down to us from aloft. He was acting like an ape.

'Little monkey!' I muttered to Skipper, as we brushed yet more snow off our backs.

Mother kept trying her best to stifle anguished cries. Dad had almost reached Scamper, coaxing him to keep still.

'Gee, Dad, this is great fun isn't...' Thud!

Scamper lay there, in front of us. His eyes were closed. His body twitched and shook. He seemed to have a little smile on his face. In seconds, Dad was beside us squatting close to Scamper.

Mum, still in the same place where Dad left her, was beside herself with grief. She wailed over and over again, unable to move. 'Oh Sam! What have we done? What have we done?'

Dad looked stunned. He cast a quick glance at us, a worried look at Mum, and then, with remorse in his brown eyes, he stared down at Scamper. Suddenly, as though driven by an alien force, he seemed to sum up the situation and commanded, 'Skipper, Springer. Come on!'

He headed towards Mum and we followed. Tears were streaming down her grey face.

'Skipper. I'm leaving you in charge,' Dad ordered. 'You take Springer and your mother home while I see to Scamper. Come on, move! There is no time to lose.'

Dad walked with us as far as the fence, consoling Mum as we went. He urged us on: 'Go on. Off with you!'

Just then, we heard a voice so familiar to us all. This usually pleasant, encouraging voice carried a note of panic to our ears.

'Oh! Scamper! Whatever has happened?'

With that, we watched helplessly as the lady crouched down by the side of Scamper's still body. Slowly, gently, she picked him up and cradled him in her arms. As she looked about the garden, we saw the same glint in her eyes that we had seen before, when there were cats about. She examined Scamper's limp body for bites, blood or any other tell-tale signs. Of course, she found none.

With Scamper nestled in her arms, the lady walked off towards the house.

Dad ushered, coaxed and led us home through the snow which suddenly had lost all its appeal. After much deliberation and discussion, Mother calmed down to such an extent that she began to have a soothing, calming effect on the rest of us. She nodded confidently to Dad and then took us in her arms and comforted us.

'Now, don't worry, dears. Scamper is in good hands. Remember when your father injured his leg?'

For all that, we couldn't help worrying. We felt so sorry for Scamper. Skipper and I were filled with remorse for having plagued our parents to let us go out to play. It was twilight before we were able to rejoice. The all-familiar voice echoes in our ears, even now.

'Sa-am! Sally! Come on! Get this little Scamp of yours. Come on! Sally! Sam!'

Skipper and I were going to rush off to meet Scamper, but Mum held us back. 'Your father will get him! And I bet you a pound of peanuts that even the lady could have told you three this morning that it was far too dangerous for young squirrels to be clambering about on slippery, snow-laden boughs and branches.'

Four-and-Twenty Starlings

Throughout the year, I put out food for the birds. How many feeds they get depends on the weather of course, and the time of year. During this very cold spell, with the ground frozen to a depth of about 8 inches, I have put out four to five plates full of oats, currants, bread, rice and pieces of fat. I change the water almost as many times, or as often as it freezes.

Have you ever noticed how greedy the starlings are? A whole flock of them descended on the patio the other day, about 24 of them. It only took them minutes to peck up the food. They were like miniature vacuum cleaners. Robins, thrushes, tits, sparrows, finches, blackbirds and doves tried to get in on the act but seemed to be intimidated by the sheer number of starlings, which were noisy and unruly, to say the least. The regulars looked quite put out. It was, after all, their food the starlings were scoffing.

Scamper watched this intrusion from the smaller of the two boxes in the oak and looked set to intervene. He didn't take his usual straight run from oak to patio. Instead, he skipped across the lawn and approached the area by way of the path running in front of the shrub border.

Whoosh! With a great fluttering of wings, much chattering, twittering, annoyed clicks and irate whistling, the colourful, slender, shimmering, speckled mimics took to their wings. Perhaps in their eagerness to fill their bellies before nightfall, they thought that Scamper was a cat. Was it my imagination, or did Scamper really look rather pleased with himself as he retreated back to the box, with two peanuts in his mouth?

I prepared another plateful of food for my regulars. It was, after all, teatime for my feathered friends.

For the moment though, they were far too busy. There was

much chirping, twittering, peeping, cooing and whistling all round. It seemed to me as though the birds were discussing the cheeky starlings' behaviour. At the same time it sounded like a dawn chorus in reverse. Was this, then, the twilight chorus? Or were the birds singing their thanks to Scamper, heralding him the hero of the day?

A little while later. Scamper retired to his drey. The birds, after finishing their evening meal, settled down for the night, and the day became another page in my garden annals.

Hills in the Garden

Last year, Digger made a real nuisance of himself in next door's garden. As fast as John flattened an earthy mound on his lawn, another would appear. One weekend, more than a dozen mole-hills sprang up overnight. Eventually after several days of no further underground digging, John dispersed the spare soil and the following weekend mowed the lawn.

For the rest of the year only one more rounded mound was pushed up from beneath. Digger it seems, has moved. Yes, you have guessed where he has taken up residence. In my garden, would you believe!

The other morning, after I got up, I looked out the window, as I usually do, to see which of the squirrels and birds were about. Instead of birds or squirrels, there, to the side of the oak and next to the path, was a huge molehill.

The day before had been sunny and quite mild. I made full use of this bonus day and dug up a huge rose tree, which had reached an enormous height, between the fence and the side of the house. Unfortunately, while in full bloom, the roses had been hidden behind some tall shrubs. I had made up my mind, last autumn, to transfer the tree to the rose garden. It turned out to be a major operation, but I managed to achieve my goal with the help of my husband. I also planted two new rose bushes which I had bought a few days before.

Opposite the rose garden was the molehill. I scooped up the soil and scattered it around the newly planted rose stocks.

I flattened and firmed the area which had been the molehill, with the back of the spade. The very next morning there was a huge mound further down. Later, while I was sitting in the lounge watching the activities in the garden, I noticed a magpie, a robin and a blackbird standing around the molehill. Digger was busy below the surface, and as he shovelled up yet more soil, with it came tasty morsels for the waiting birds.

A few feet from the hill and the birds, I saw a goldfinch. I wanted a closer look at this colourful bird and reached for the binoculars. There, I had it in view! How handsome it looked. Without warning the finch was lifted by the lawn. The bird flew off to the bottom of the lawn to join the others of its kind. The magpie flapped a hasty retreat too but the robin and blackbird stayed close to the large mound and were soon joined by a thrush. Even as I watched the spot where the goldfinch had stood, the mound of soil erupted from below the hardened surface of the lawn. The fresh soil grew into a bigger dome by the minute.

Other birds arrived on the scene, eager to pick up anything this wintry soil had to offer. Equipped with a spade, I made my way to the miniature volcano and stood over it, watching its eruption with intrigue for a few minutes. As the cold got the better of me, I shovelled up the loose earth and finally whacked the back of the spade on the two soft spots.

The top lawn will never be in contention with a bowling green because the intricate, widespread root systems of the aged oak saps up all the nourishment and moisture. I accept that. However, having molehills sprouting up all over the lawn will do nothing to help, encourage or enhance its appearance.

I like to watch the comings and goings in the garden, but as far as possible, I think that I will discourage visits from Digger in the future.

Spring Fever

It is still only the middle of January. The winter has been cold and damp so far. In spite of this, the first green tips of the spring flowers, under the great oak and in front of the holly, have been above the ground since before Christmas.

Last Sunday, it was sunny, quite mild and dry enough for me to rake up the soggy leaves. The rose garden, shrub border and the top lawn were ankle-deep in sycamore, oak and ash leaves. Later, when I had completed the back-breaking task I had set myself, I inspected the garden. Spring seems to be following in the wake of the snow. The magnolia tree, I noticed with delight, is already heavy with buds. The honeysuckle is covered with green tips and the lilac bush is bursting with swollen buds. There is much evidence of new life around me.

All of last year's offspring are regular visitors to the garden patio and even the lounge!

Blacky and Sooty's five chicks, who survived the onslaught of next door's cats last year, are in good condition. Hoppy keeps himself to himself. As soon as he thinks the coast is clear, he comes out of hiding from around the side of the house, onto the patio. No sooner has he pecked a few beaksful of breakfast, dinner or tea when, from nowhere, it seems, his own kind swoop down to join him, chasing him off more often than not. Poor Hoppy!

Young Spotter, whose parents were both killed on the day of the ambush, is faring well. He made friends with a number of other thrushes. I can't remember seeing more than one pair last year.

Perhaps news has got around by 'word of beak' that there is a constant supply of food on the patio!

Many of the finches, tits, sparrows, robins and blackbirds, and the two doves, were all reared within the garden and its perimeter. Even as I am writing, the garden is alive with chirping, flapping, singing birds.

Sam and Sally I have not seen for several weeks now. They are obviously leaving the garden free to their three youngsters, knowing that they will be well looked after, with affection and endless supply of nuts. I do wish, though, that the old couple would put in an appearance from time to time, just for me to see that they are all right. I wonder how Sam's leg is. Some of the cats are still a problem and persecute the birds and the squirrels. Deep down, I am sure that Skipper, Springer and Scamper, and all the birds, know that I am on their side. As soon as I see the squirrels twitching their tails in an agitated manner, or hear the birds screeching angrily, I am outside like a flash, chasing away an offending feline.

Just now, one little sparrow flew past with a long piece of dry grass in its beak. It really does seem a bit early for nest building. Perhaps it is only a trial run, putting into practice what its parents have taught it. A few of the birds are already pairing off. Last year's two young doves have stuck together like glue. Where one flies or coos, the other is never far behind.

The thrushes and blackbirds have begun their courtship and more and more they seem to be flying around in couples. Perhaps, this spring, some of my bird boxes will be put to good use.

The fight for supremacy and leadership has long been resolved by the squirrels. Skipper is definitely the reigning monarch and King of the Castle, or rather the big box, high up on the trunk of the oak. The perilous chases through the trees, at break-neck speeds, seem to be less frequent now.

The trio still have the odd mad five minutes but once that is out of their system, they settle down and get on quite well. One at a time they collect nuts from the ledge of the patio door, leap across the lawn, scrabble up the trunk of the oak and find their favourite place to sit and nibble.

When, inadvertently, I have not been keeping an eye on the

nuts and all of them have been devoured, Scamper is usually the first to point this out. He sits on the ledge. Inside he can see a bowl full of nuts. With his nose and front paws pressed against the glass he looks as though he is trying to push the panes inward. Oh! The frustration! A quick flick of his tail, in the hope of attracting my attention, hopping, sniffing here and there and finally, success. Point taken! I put out more nuts and call out, 'Come on then,' and Scamper responds. Little he may be but he has perfected the art of cramming two and even three peanuts into his mouth. He usually eats one and buries the other one or two, which accounts for all the nuts I raked up with the leaves last week.

Scamper, although the smallest of the trio, is absolutely fearless, even to the point of defying the slippery, snow-laden oak branches which resulted in his fall from a great height. He has no inhibitions either. He often comes into the lounge and helps himself to nuts. The other day, after he had nibbled his way through the shells of three or four peanuts, he decided to have a look around.

With his back legs spread wide, he crouched his way behind the settee, around the armchair, through the lounge and into the dining room. There he jumped up onto the settee, explored it, and then started a preening ritual. Only when he was quite satisfied that his face was clean, his ears and body well scratched and his tail fluffed up to a squirrel's standard, he decided it was time for some more nuts.

For the sake of watching these cute little creatures, I would gladly leave the door open more often. Invariably, the weather is too harsh at this time of year. The biting air rushes in through even the smallest gap.

Lucky

The garden was blanketed in a dull grey twilight of a winter's evening. The birds sounded disturbed in their finale of the day. I guessed that a cat was behind their noisy, shrill cries. Several minutes passed and the anger in their throats quietened. A male and female blackbird, a song thrush and a robin hopped, pecked and scratched about under the small holly bush growing at the side of the oak. Even though the ground was hard, it looked as though the birds managed to find grubs amongst the leaves.

I saw movement behind one of the stones in the rockery. It was the new cat from over the other side. Black and white, with a smart blue collar. A handsome-looking animal, but still a cat. He looked full of hunter and killer instincts. I had seen him on several occasions and each time he had been up to no good. He's obviously never heard of 'live and let live'. Danger!

The black and white job crouched low and snaked his way through the heathers, across the path and round the back of the oak. Three birds flew off. I saw the wings of the fourth flapping in a struggle to get away. The cat pawed into the lower growth of the holly. I dashed across the lawn, and when I was level with the left side of the oak, I came face to face with the cat. I heard a plaintive pathetic peep out of the jaws of the black and white hunter. I yelled at him, 'Drop it!'

Surprised by the unwelcomed confrontation, the cat arched his back and hissed and spat with great annoyance, and an even more surprised blackbird rolled out of the jaws of death. The cat made off along the bank of the stream. The bird found his wings and flapped a few yards to the safety of the holly bush.

He was the first to arrive for breakfast the next morning. His close encounter with death has ruffled and damaged a few feathers at the top of his left leg. He has joined the ranks of the other birds with definite distinguishing marks and has thus acquired a name, too. Under the circumstances, I think 'Lucky' is a very appropriate name for him.

The Fury of February

It is the first time for years that I have not been able to pick daffodils in time for St David's Day. There again, in the previous garden, I had beautiful Tenby daffodils, which flower long before the others. In the milder conditions, prior to this ruthless last month, nature had pushed well ahead in her bid towards the completion of her annual cycle to produce spring flowers. The daffodils have advanced only marginally since their first green tips teased through the ground. The leaves of the snowdrops are keeping their little heads tightly covered, reluctant to expose their delicate faces to the force of the winds.

The garden looks drab and barren, the grass sapped of its colour. New bud shoots are frozen on their stems and branches. Leaves of evergreen shrubs are dried and curled up, rustling in the relentless east wind. The rhododendron leaves have lost their usually glossy finish and hang like limp, dirty rags. Any effort to rekindle them fails again and again, as the fury of the icy wind hurls away any warmth the sun might have to offer. The lack of rain has made grass, heath and gorse tracts vulnerable to countless fires. It is as though growth and time has stopped, while the jaws of the frost hold the land in a vice-like grip.

Neither man nor nature is accustomed to the harshness of this weather, which has enveloped these, our isles, this February.

A Bird is a Bird is a Bird?

I am very fond of garden birds. With regular feeding, I am able to observe them up close, which gives me endless enjoyment.

There are about a dozen blackbirds which never fly too far from the garden. Seeing six, eight or more of them at the same time, in close proximity, one could be forgiven for assuming that they are all the same. Other than the obvious difference of male and female colouring of feathers and beaks, they are all very much individuals.

Hoppy immediately springs to mind. His right leg is at a peculiar angle to his body. The thigh looks as though it has been pulled away from the flank. When in flight, Hoppy displays a bare, red patch at the top of his leg. He doesn't seem to suffer too much discomfort and manages to hobble about at a right rate of knots. Having said that, the very cold weather does seem to bother him.

A few days ago I noticed a blackbird hen with a bad left foot. The slightest pressure or weight on it seems agony for her. She lands a little one-sidedly and immediately tucks her injured foot under her body. While feeding on the patio, she hops about on one leg. Maybe she and Hoppy ought to get together.

Another hen, although similar to the others, seems to have been blessed with a much richer brown plumage and she has far more pronounced dark, almost black, spots on her chest. This makes her look quite different and she certainly stands out from the rest. Besides, I have special interest in Baby, victim of the ambush.

There are dozens of different finches and sparrows, all far too busy to keep still long enough to be studied for individuality. However, of the chaffinches there is one noticeable exception: Podgy!

If you have been lucky enough to observe the colourful little finches, you will have noticed that the slate blue head of the male runs into brown down the neck and back, shading to olive on his rump. While feeding, the rump is not really visible. This is what foxed me when I first saw Podgy. I knew he was a chaffinch and yet I had never noticed one with such a lovely olive green rump! Slimline finches fold their wings tidily across their backs, hiding any traces of olive-coloured feathers.

Podgy, on the other hand, is fat, round and looks like a coloured dumpling. Because of his unconventional size, he has trouble getting his wings tucked around his middle and neatly folded across his back. So, his olive rump is permanently on display. Podgy doesn't venture too far and conserves his flying energy for when an absolute need for it arises. For most of the day he hops around on the lawn, feeds on the patio and often just sits and watches the comings and goings. Even when I open the door, he makes no attempt to fly off. That effort is reserved for any cats that might be prowling around, or to settle down for the night.

Scruffy and Tatty hatched five magpie chicks last year. Unlike their parents, they are all beautifully turned out and a credit to their mother and father. Scruffy has a distinctive patch of tiny black feathers on his otherwise, snowy white breast and belly, giving the appearance of a grey smudge on his chest or as if wearing a medal. Somehow, he always looks unwashed. Tatty, Scruffy's mate and mother to their young, has a couple of feathers sticking out where feathers oughtn't to stick out. All the preening and wing-flapping doesn't seem to make the slightest difference to improving her overall appearance. No matter how hard she tries, she always looks tatty.

One of the four resident robins is much smaller and slimmer than the others. Two of them are virtually identical. Shirty, is definitely the odd one out. From the top of his wings, that is, from the lesser wing coverts to the median wing coverts, just below, a little white feather sticks out on either side. This makes him look like a young man about town, all dressed up but with his waistcoat or shirt unbuttoned and flapping in the breeze. That is why he is called Shirty. Other robins have these little white feathers too, but somehow they always seem to manage to keep them neatly tucked in.

Bossy is still about but Gaffer, another blackbird, is putting in his bid for supremacy. He has thought up a way of getting the lion's share of the food I put out. If not the lion's share, then certainly the pick of it. He seems to know precisely when I am about to throw out food. Gaffer is there, on the fence, waiting.

As soon as I have closed the door again, he makes the most terrible din, yelling and clucking noisily. The other birds take heed of 'Look out, there's a cat!' and take to their wings to fly to loftier heights. And Gaffer calmly descends onto the patio and greedily feasts on crumbs an currants, clucking as he pecks, with much satisfaction.

The sparrows, finches, robins and starlings are usually the first to realise that whatever danger Gaffer had warned them about, has gone and they quickly join him. One by one, seeing all the other birds on the patio in apparent safety, the other blackbirds emerge from hiding, protesting loudly at having been had, yet again!

One of last year's starling offspring looks really comical. Clown – that's his name – has all the makings of an actor or a Big Top performer. Where make-up is concerned, he has really gone to town with the stuff. His head is quite grey, and amid this unusual starling colouring, his eyes are surrounded by black patches which take up most of the sides of his face. He looks as if he has dabbled with a sample of black paint or used mascara rather excessively or even just stepped out of a boxing ring after 15 hard rounds with a mightier opponent.

The resident doves, with their thin ring across the back of their necks, look quite elegant as they graciously stroll across the lawn. There are two doves which sometimes come into the garden to visit or for a quick snack. One of them has a much wider collar which ends in a roundish patch either side of its neck. This makes it look as though the dove's personal headphones have slipped to the side of its neck. I wonder if you can guess why this dove is called DJ.

One of the wood pigeons has a damaged wing. It has no problems when flying, from what I have seen, but while it is on the ground it looks as though it is carrying a briefcase or a brolly, or something under its wing. Despite this obvious injury, which only happened within the last two months or so, Porter always tries to look as dignified as possible.

Not immediately obvious is the injured or malformed foot of one of the song thrushes. On her left foot, her outer, middle and inner toes seem to be curled downward and her hind toe never touches the ground. Although there is an obvious disfigurement, Ballerina seems to get by quite well.

During my observations of the bird life in my garden, I have logged 38 different species. Eleven of these I had never seen before, or if I have, I had not looked closely enough to appreciate their colour, sex or plumage.

Next time you put out food for your garden birds, take a good look. See how many differences you can spot amongst your regular feathered visitors. After all, one bird is not just another bird.

Mad March

The freezing, Arctic-like weather of the past couple of months is a thing of the past. After the first quarter of the month, March has brought with it much milder conditions. Although I have roses to plant and need to give the garden a general tidy up, I feel loath to do so at present.

There is a constant flurry of activity from the birds. There seem to be more than ever. The garden resembles a huge open-air aviary, set in a natural environment, which boasts many bird species, including male and female blackcaps, great spotted and green woodpeckers, waxwings, jays and redwings. One of the great spotted is getting to feel quite at home and comes onto the patio to feed. Even without his beautiful colouring, his distinctive shape and stance would make it easy to spot him, even in a crowd.

At last, the dainty little snowdrops have uncovered their faces and the crocuses have added a splash of colour to the base of the oak. The daffodils are pushing up well but even now, with only ten days of March left, there is still no sign of any bloom.

The doves mated on the 11th and again on the 13th and on both occasions they spent the next 15 minutes or so sitting side by side, rubbing necks and beaks and being generally very loving towards each other.

Last year's sparrows' nest under the corner of the roof tiles, Blacky and Sooty's nest, and one or two others have been refurbished by new owners. There is a lot of building material being flown to and fro. Other couples are still undecided as to their perfect nesting sites. Yet, others are playing hard to get and seem in no particular hurry to choose a partner. Most of the birds, though, are going through various stages of courtship – male chasing female and vice versa, cock chasing off other cocks, who dare to encroach and display to a female with whom he believes to have something going. Strutting, displaying, the ruffling of feathers, showing off and mid-air beak fights are all part of these days when the spring spirit is welling amid the birds.

The rain has been quite welcome but the frost has taken its toll. Some of the evergreens are badly scarred, with as many brown as green or variegated leaves. The recent strong winds have dismembered some of these affected leaves from their stems and the discarded foliage along the ground of the shrubbery has given it an autumnal effect. High winds have been raging over the weekend and even the solemnity of Palm Sunday could not stem the wild gusty forces. Old, dead wood has been snapped off the branches and lies strewn across the lawns. Last night's lashing rains and high winds have flattened some of the crocuses, turning the colours of this nature's palette into an untidy mess.

There is washing to be done on this, the devil's birthday, but I have no inclination to do it. I refuse to do battle with the winds and the frequent heavy showers, still quite wintry in their content.

I wonder how secure the birds' nests are which have already been built over the last few weeks? Are they holding fast to their anchorage points? I would expect them to as we are, after all, dealing with expert builders. The garden is filled with a sort of frantic intensity.

Easter Sunday too, has been and gone now and still I haven't a single daffodil but, at least their tips are now a yellowy green. Yesterday, on the last day of March, I busied myself in the garden, pruning, planting, digging and staking. Finally, I raked the top lawn to rid it of some of the moss, empty peanut shells and pieces of dead wood fallen from the oak. This last week has been a busy one for me. I had to work for all bar one day of it, therefore, observations in the garden went down to virtually nil.

In the little spare time I had, I managed to replace several shrubs for those which had been damaged by frost. Opposite the patio door is a brand new teak bird table, which a friend of mine in Hampshire made for me. This has been well received and approved by the birds. The tits and greenfinches keep making short work of the peanuts hanging in a bag, above the patio door. It doesn't take them long to peck their way through the protein filled kernels which they do with much relish and acrobatic stunts.

Between the end of the side patio and the magnolia tree, I have strung some plastic mesh netting from the fence to two posts, to train the old climbing rose into an arch. To the right of the patio door, I lifted one of the flagstones and dug deep down to get out all the sand and rubble and then filled the hole with last year's leaf and grass mould as well as fresh soil and peat. The yellow climbing rose flanked by red ones should make a spectacular show in the summer months.

I have also sown sweet peas, Chinese lanterns, sunflowers, herbs and nasturtiums and I am keeping my fingers crossed and hope to inhale the sweet smells of success in a couple of months.

It's been quite a hectic, mad sort of month.

April the First

The great spotted woodpecker brought along a mate to the patio this morning and showed it where the food was. Four of the robins have paired off and a couple of mistle thrushes spent the best part of an hour trying out possible nest sites in the oak trunk which has grown at an angle of about 45 degrees and is well covered in ivy. The hen was particularly exciting to watch as she explored this fork of a branch, then that one, settling down, spreading her wings and standing up again to look about her. She followed her mate from site to site as he, too, went through the imaginary motion of brooding.

It is the sort of morning that makes me glad to be alive, grateful for sight and hearing, and most appreciative of my beautiful surroundings. Well, between making various observations, reading my mail and writing, it is about time for elevenses – which the birds are already having.

Although I have plenty to do indoors, to catch up on some of the jobs which I left last week, the sunshine beckons me into the garden. I have to rake the bottom lawn gently because the bluebells are already pushing their way up. It will probably be the last chance today as I want to minimise any damage I might cause to the eventual blue carpet. The rose bed needs hoeing, and after that I must concentrate on the front garden.

Later

Isn't it funny how things work out? After a beautiful morning and an early lunch I drove to the nursery and selected some pansies, forget-me-nots, heathers, nasturtiums and two more rose bushes. By the time I had returned home with my new acquisitions, the lovely sunshine had given way to a deluge of rain, mixed with sleet and hail. My earlier enthusiasm for gardening had not waned and so, donned with a weather-proof jacket I promptly became part of all that fell on me from above, for half an hour, just long enough to plant the rose bushes and divide the other purchases between the three tubs. I am so looking forward to the later time of spring and, of course, summer. My joy is like that of a child, waiting for Christmas.

A starling pair closely inspected the big box this morning. Inside, underneath, above and even the small gap between the box and the tree trunk. Finally they decided that, although very spacious and conveniently situated to such amenities as food and water, it really wasn't quite the sort of residence they had had in mind. Had they asked, I would have advised against it too. No doubt the squirrels would not have welcomed the intrusion either. The small dunnocks are quite unassuming little things. They hop about, picking up seeds or bread from the bird table or the patio, and whoosh! They're off again.

Evening

Skipper, Springer and Scamper were in the garden the whole day and all but exhausted my supply of peanuts. They watched with intrigue while I planted the roses and filled the tubs, getting soaked to the skin. As I turned each spade full of soil, I picked out the worms and left them in a little dish on the patio. The blackbirds, robin and song thrushes had them for their tea. Despite the terrific showers this afternoon and the fact that I had to resign myself to doing some more washing, it has been such a beautiful day in so many ways.

More of April

April has never had a good reputation as far as the weather is concerned. This year, though, must surely be the worst on record. Following in the wake of many other record-breaking conditions of last winter, we are still being snowed, rained, hailed and sleeted upon, and tossed about by icy, marrow-chilling, gusty gales. And this is already the end of the first week of April.

I have seen clumps of daffodils out and about, in parks and on the verges, which have started to bloom, regretfully perhaps from their 'point of flower', considering the nasty weather they are facing. Nature as well as humans may well have been fooled by early spells of spring-like sunshine. My daffodils are still refusing to show their yellow faces to the world. In many ways, they might yet be the best weather guides in my garden.

The food I put out for the birds is received as eagerly now as it was during the hardest frost and snow.

I have managed to spend some time in the garden while the sun was out for brief periods. I have extended the rose garden, yet again! There are planted tubs either side of the big patio door. These created quite a lot of interest by birds and squirrels alike. One of the great tits landed on the rim of one tub, stretched itself to its utmost extent, looked at all the plants, hopped through them and then flew off. Within a minute it was back with another tit. This one repeated what the first one had done. After a full inspection it joined its friend on the rim and it looked almost as though it nodded with approval as the first seemed to say, 'See, it's nice, isn't it?'

The great tits, greenfinches and blue tits frequent the new bird table, not so much to feed on but as a take-off base towards the peanut bag above the patio door. All of them like to play 'I'm the King of the Castle' (or rather the peanut bag), by spreading their wings, fanning out their tails and emitting a soft but raspy snake-like sound to any other who dares to approach, hissing 'Get off, I was here first!'

At first I thought the great tits and siskin to be more tolerant than the blue tits. Not so, however. On further observation I found that each time it is a case of first come, first served. While waiting its turn to get onto the bag, a blue or great tit might take off with one of the squirrels' nuts off the door ledge, leaving me wondering how little things like that can take off with such loads, let alone remain in flight.

The two coconut halves on the oak are enjoyed by both tits and squirrels. One of the halves already has a stick pushed through the flesh and one of the 'eyes', ready for when the last of the white nut has been pecked or gnawed away, so that I can fill it with liquid fat and titbits, and once solidified, it can be hung out again as a special treat for the colourful little acrobats. Because the nut halves are hanging upside down, the squirrels look particularly funny as they grip tightly into the tree bark with their hind legs and manipulate the nut with their front paws. When their small heads disappear inside the brown shell, it makes me think of a little child trying on its parent's hats which fit it perfectly, down to the chin and neck!

It is a dull, grey, damp day and cold, much more akin to November or January, rather than April. Despite the poor growing conditions, there are lots more shoots, leaf tips and germinating seeds in evidence.

A couple of days ago, it wasn't a case of tip-toeing through the tulips but among the bluebell leaves on the bottom lawn to gather the twigs and dead wood. I decided to do the job by hand rather than use the lawn rake as the growth of the blue bells is already too advanced to be subjected to the steel prongs, which would have done untold damage. The new growth all around has given the drab winter garden a whole new image. It will be quite some time yet before all the trees are clad in leaves once more.

In the meantime, even the bare silhouettes of deciduous giants add a special something to the garden and to the mysteries of nature.

Aha! Missed Me!

On Sundays, I usually hang out new peanut bags or just top them up. I have invested in a second one which I have suspended on the bird table, hammock-style.

For some reason, the first quarter of the one hanging above the door always seems to go down the quickest. It probably isn't so much that the top part gets eaten quicker but that the weight of the nuts, movement and gravity settles them and packs them tightly to the bottom.

By the time I had distributed food on the patio and the bird table for the next morning, for the early birds, and a handful of peanuts for the squirrels, pulled the blinds and drawn the curtains, I noticed that the bag of peanuts was three-quarters full.

Imagine my surprise the next morning, when I saw the bag

half empty already. Regardless of what time I get up in the morning, my first job is to feed the birds and the squirrels. Anything I have put out the night before, or whatever has been left after they have finished their tea, is quickly eaten up in the early hours.

It wasn't until I was drinking my coffee that the mystery of the vanishing nuts was solved. Up until then, the usual tits and finches had squabbled and vied for the best position on the suspended bags. The wing spreading, tail fanning and 'hissing' went on until, whoosh! Two blue tits, a great tit and a greenfinch took off simultaneously and – enter the culprit! None other than Woody. The great spotted woodpecker made a perfect landing on the vertically suspended bag and for a full ten minutes he clung there and pecked away as though peanuts were about to be struck off the menu for good. His much larger beak not only succeeded in getting more nuts out through the fine nylon mesh but he also ripped the netting. Several nuts fell on the ground, bounced and rolled amongst the food on the patio. For these nuts there were immediate takers.

As soon as Woody had eaten what, for the time being, he considered to be an elegant sufficiency, the smaller birds returned. They were quick to realise that now there was one much larger opening, and they were able to peck out whole nuts and fly off with them to eat on a fence or in a bush.

I watched Woody's dexterity, as he clung to the bag, on and off for an hour. I even walked right up to the door, and with nothing but double glazing between us, the two of us eyed each other. My presence did not deter him. He looked every inch a clown, compared to the usual acrobats, all dressed up in his bright, colourful plumage.

Why hadn't I thought of it before? If he tolerated my nearness, I could take a photograph! I rushed upstairs for our 'idiot-proof' camera. That was an obvious mistake. I sat or stood, poised for two hours, camera switched on and ready for action. Nothing! This beautiful bird wasn't just a clown, he was also a thought reader and obviously camera-shy. Perhaps my patience will be rewarded soon so that I will be able to add a photograph of Woody to my collection of birds, squirrels and garden photographs.

Observations

Many of us could be accused of looking without actually seeing or registering what we are looking at. How often we trundle through town, maybe the same town, to do our shopping or go about our business, heads down to shield us from the weather and to watch where we are stepping. How enlightening it is to look up once in a while to see the tops of buildings, facades we never knew were there, steeples, towers, signs and skylines – even the clouds present us with ever-changing spectacles. The world becomes a different, more magical place when we look with open eyes.

It is much like that with the garden, too. When one has the same view every day, one tends to take in the overall picture and forget about the shady nooks and the wonderful powers of nature that lie therein. Perhaps we take too much for granted.

My awareness of what is around me is far greater now than ever it was, although I have always been one for looking about me. As far as possible, I like to walk around the garden at least once a day. Although not always instantly recognisable, there are changes taking place all the time. As one cycle nears completion, the next one is only just beginning. Yesterday's tiny bud is fractionally bigger today; the constant force of nature, striving to fulfil her part.

In an earlier chapter, I mentioned that the sparrows and tits never seem to stay still long enough to study closely. With the help of the peanut bags, I have been able to look much closer at the tits, in particular. I am quite amazed at all the variations in their markings which makes them far more individual than I had thought.

Just like Chubby, one of the chaffinches, there is a little round ball of feathers amongst the great tits. Tubby looks like a multicoloured powder puff. He stands out exceptionally well. Other tits, I have learned to differentiate by their markings, especially those from the neck to the belly. Some have wide black bands running from the neck down to between their legs, almost retaining the width of the band all the way down. Others start off broad and taper to a narrow line of feathers. Yet others look as though they are wearing outsize cravats or old-fashioned wide ties. One of these little chaps looks quite handsome with his neat collar which runs as a thin line just down to his belly. This gives Dapper a sort of well-dressed appearance, as though he is wearing a black shirt under a rather smart, yellow jacket. A few of the blue tits sport nothing more than a black collar over their yellow vests.

A recent newcomer to the bird table, peanut bags and patio is a little blue tit, much smaller even – if that is possible – than all the others. This one has a broad white stripe from the back of his head to his nape. Apart from this unusual difference, the poor little mite only has one leg. I can't help feeling that Brucy at some time or other had designs on being a pirate.

All these little differences are quite intriguing and certainly an eye-opener.

Starry's Passing

Mid-morning, while sitting in the armchair by the patio door, from where I can observe most of the back garden and its activities, one of the many starlings came, half waddling, half lumbering from the bottom lawn across the top one. The bird dragged its right, badly damaged, wing. Slowly, painfully, it made its way to the patio, tossed a few pieces of bread about and eventually had two currants and a drink of water. It hobbled to the shrub border where it tried to make itself inconspicuous. An attempt to get itself off ground level by trying, repeatedly, to half hop into the lowest fork of one of the evergreens, about 6 inches off the ground, failed miserably.

In agony and badly shaken it hobbled on, occasionally trying a one-winged take-off, needless to say without success. Still looking for a place to hide, it crossed the herb garden. Behind a couple of the big stones which surround the earthy patch, it hid. Exhausted after its cumbersome excursion, it sat there for an hour or more, too weak to move, oblivious of any dangers that might be lurking.

A sense of survival took over and again the starling made its way towards the patio, but this time, along the path separating the shrubbery from the top lawn. Halfway along the path, the bird all but keeled over. In its agonising stupor, it unwittingly toppled sideways and ended up leaning against the stones which form the edging and retain the soil in the border. In vain, it tried to utilise its damaged wing to right itself. In despair for a foothold, it shuffled about and after a hard struggle it all but managed to straighten itself, but still lolling, needing the stones for support. The bird leaned against there and rested. Its will to survive far exceeded its capabilities. A warning call from a magpie and a blackbird screeched through the air. The starling responded. With all its might and the little strength it had left it tried desperately to climb the two layers of stones which had propped it up. Though no more than 9 inches high, to the starling the top of the stones must have seemed like Ben Nevis.

I too had heard the warning. As there was a great rush of wings from the side of the garden to the right, I knew where to look for the danger. As soon as I saw the black and white menace, I tossed a stone towards it. The hard object ricocheted off the oak, about 12 feet away from the cat, but the noise was enough to let Minstrel know that he was not welcome.

Back in my armchair I pondered what to do for the best, regarding the injured bird. Other starlings swooped noisily onto the patio and the bird table with not a care in the world. Two of them waddled to the injured party and mercilessly pecked it several times before they flew off. This helped little towards the bird's injuries, its feeble state or its pride. I decided that enough was enough. If his own kind treated it with such contempt, what chance did the poor thing have to put up a fight against a real predator?

In the garage I found a box. I lined the bottom with a plastic bag and topped this with several layers of newspaper. Out of the pedal bin I picked an empty milk carton and cut across the top and bottom to leave me with two, approximately 1 inch high trays, one for water, the other for bread and currants. With the trays in position I carried the box to the lounge and set it down by the door. The patio was alive with birds. It was lunchtime, after all. I didn't want to frighten them away or interrupt their lunch and decided to wait until something would make them swoop off.

While watching them feeding, the bickering over the same piece of bread, the fights and the intimidations, I witnessed one of the most extraordinary scenes I have ever seen or am ever likely to see again.

A little robin, which I had earlier seen hopping about the injured bird, picked up a currant and flew over to the incapacitated starling. There it dropped the currant in front of the bird. The Samaritan repeated this procedure three times. The starling tried its best to lower its head so that its beak could reach the precious offerings. This exercise obviously required far more strength and balance than the bird possessed.

Then, just as I thought of putting my home-from-home box into good use, the starling moved. Painfully it hopped along the path and found one section of stones lower than the level of the rest, and managed to get onto the shrub border. It wobbled and reeled before it finally settled in the new growth of a clump of marguerites.

I couldn't sit back and watch this suffering any longer. Besides, the bird was a sitting duck for some of the cats which sometimes came into the garden between the right side of the house and the fence, where the shrubbery begins. I went outside and gently spoke to the bird. Its eyelids were heavy and its breathing laboured. Without any struggling or change in its heart rate, it allowed me to pick it up.

In its new home I managed to coax it to eat a couple of currants and to drink some water. It slept and rested for lengthy spells. Every time I heard the paper rustle I crouched down by the box and talked to Starry again, coaxing him to eat, drink, rest and get better. For a while, I really thought that Starry was showing signs of improvement. Alas! At four-thirty that afternoon, he stretched his good wing and his legs for the last time.

I felt that, at least, he had spent his last few hours in relative comfort, warmth and away from danger.

Half an hour later, I buried Starry in the rose garden in the hope that he would become a bird of paradise.

Halfway Through April

It has been raining all night and now at eight o'clock in the morning, thick grey clouds are hanging low and it still looks just like first light. Since dawn, the graceful, elegant mistle thrush pair have been back and forth to their chosen nest site countless times. There is a copse of five trees near the edge of the stream. The mistle thrushes picked one of these which has a thick growth of ivy clinging to its trunk. Halfway up this trunk, just about where the ivy growth ends, the couple are setting up home.

The collared doves and a magpie are showing a keen interest in the mistle thrushes' home and each time one of the doves or the magpie ventures too close to the nest it gets an unceremonious send-off. An angry pursuit follows, a flying chase down the gully of the stream or through trees and bushes.

The doves mated on the 13th and several times since then, a month after DJ and his chosen one bonded their union. Despite the amorous courtship, I have seen no evidence of nest material being sought. For a couple of days last week, the doves were in a strange mood. They fought and pecked at each other. One wouldn't allow the other on the table to feed without getting all flustered and its feathers ruffled. Whatever their differences were, they seem to have sorted them out and are cooing, necking, beak-rubbing and feeding again, side by side.

It is still quite early in the morning and Scamper has already been chased by a cat, which, as soon as it saw me, beat a hasty retreat. In his dash to the top of the fence and safety, Scamper dropped the peanut on to the lawn which only seconds before he had taken off the door ledge. He was still sitting on the fence, flicking his tail, the way he does when threatened. I opened the door and called to him, assuring him that the cat had gone.

Instantly he scrabbled down the fence, across the rose bed, the path and the lawn to the very spot where his nut lay. He sat there and nibbled it just as though nothing had happened.

Two of the blackbirds are dividing their time between breakfasting and nest building. They have chosen a site somewhere in the overgrown scrub of next door's garden. The usual colourful flock is assembled on the patio for breakfast, and it looks as though it is about time I put out a second helping of everything.

Having said that the doves had shown no interest in nest building, one of them has since picked up a few long strands of weeds and some thin twigs, which it rolled about in its beak and promptly discarded again. The days pass quickly when they are filled with lots of interesting things to see, do and write about.

Now, at teatime, the patio is as busy as it was this morning, and at midday. This must have been a popular day for mating. The nest was completed by lunchtime, and between twelve and twelve-thirty the mistle thrushes became one. Three, four times the mate visited the female, in quick succession. Then he flew to a neighbouring tree and preened himself for ages with his back turned to his mate, almost as though he did not know her. She, in the meantime, remained on the branch of her tree, twitching and flapping her wings, trying her best to attract her lover's attention again to show him that she was still receptive.

For a couple of hours this afternoon all the birds – and there must have been best part of 200 – seemed as though they had all been wound up and the keys thrown away. The lawns, all the trees, shrubs and bushes were absolutely alive with birds, chasing each other, flying high, diving low, swooping and turning tight circles. Woody too, with his intended, took part in the pursuit rituals. Amid all this, a sparrow couple mated in an apple tree next door, while all around them the break-neck flights of fancy carried on. No doubt quite a few of the birds found their ideal partners today.

Helping Nature

April is probably the month which can boast most bird activity in the garden. Consequently it offers far more variety, behaviour and material to write about.

Some of the starlings have decided that the long dry leaves of the pampas grass make ideal building material. I have watched them playing tug-of-war with these dead, yet strong, fibres and trying to fly off with one, while the end of the strand is still firmly attached to the main plant, resulting in an abrupt, unexpected crash landing. Having taken to their wings they don't seem to have the sense to just let go of the grass. On the whole, the starlings seem to lack common sense, which they display time and again when feeding. With all the bread on the patio, there are always three or four of them who have to fight over one piece. Any piece of crust will change beaks quite a few times before the strongest of the group manages to get away with it or the bread is scooped up by a finch or a sparrow, leaving the starlings to enact another battle over another piece of bread. In the name of progress and nature, I have cut the dead pampas leaves. Having all but called the starlings thick, they have been quick to take advantage of this trimmed and ready-made material.

Baby and her partner are making use of the strawberry runners to mould their nest. I have started to throw out the flat wedges of fluff which accumulate in the mesh filter inside the tumble dryer. These downy-soft pieces are quickly gathered by some birds which have realised the potential of this snug waste product.

A couple of days ago I cleared the bottom lawn where it slopes down to the stream. Most of this area was being choked by yards and yards of bramble runners, winding their way around trees, holly and ivy and strangling nettles and daffodils, weeds and the wild flowers which will soon bloom there. I treaded and looked carefully for signs of nests. Luckily I did not disturb anything. Fortunately, the soil is soft and I was able to pull the long, thorny snakes out by their roots. There is a huge pile of these, together with dead wood and branches which, when dried out, I'll be able to burn. The soil in the dell is rich and black. Years of fallen leaves have rotted into a fertile patch of ground.

I had finished uprooting the brambles and then raked the area before going indoors. Within minutes there was a mass exodus of finches, starlings, robins and blackbirds from the top garden to the cleared site, to feast on grubs and worms which I had disturbed and unearthed. The side lawn I have now dug up completely, and planted a few more rose bushes. At last the whole area has become a rose bed, apart from the magnolia tree which has been there for some years.

During each day the sparrows hold frequent meetings, the favourite venue being the magnolia. These assemblies tend to be noisy, disorderly affairs with all the sparrows chirping at the same time and none of them getting a cheep in edgeways.

The yellow and white crocuses finished flowering weeks ago. However, the purple ones seem more robust and are only now coming to an end. About half a dozen daffodils are blooming in the dell and along the banks of the stream. I can't see these from the lounge, only from the bedroom window or if I walk towards the dell. The daffodils at the base of the oak and those in front of the holly are yellow buds and still not open. These must be late varieties. Well, at least that is my excuse for them. Who can blame them to refuse to herald the spring when just yesterday, the 21st of April, sleet and hailstones as big as peas, pelted them mercilessly?

Whenever I have been digging or raking, I have gathered the worms into a shallow dish. Without soil or moisture these wrigglers don't survive very long, and make tasty snacks for some of the birds. Any which they leave, or fat ones, I keep back, to become a supper dish for Spiky.

He has been coming onto the patio regularly lately, usually around nine o'clock. He makes a beeline for the dish and even tips it up to make sure that he hasn't missed a worm. He is quite partial to peanuts too. Last night Spiky brought along the rest of his hedgehog family. In this garden, activities certainly don't start with the dawn and end at dusk.

Night Life

Spiky, Hedgy and Prickles have become regular members of my living garden, bringing it to life during the hours of darkness. At first, they shied away from the lounge light if the curtains and blinds were drawn back. Now they have accepted the artificial light shining onto the patio, and don't object to being watched.

The hedgehogs come in three sizes. Spiky is the biggest and judging by the number of peanuts he eats, has the biggest appetite too. Hedgy is noticeably smaller, and amongst other things is quite fond of brown bread. Prickles is a mere handful and will eat anything I have left out for the spiky trio: nuts, bread, pieces of coconut, bits of meat, scraps of fat and any worms I have come across while gardening. After a long sleep and a hard winter which ran well into spring, it seems that these little creatures have built up insatiable appetites.

All this eating seems to be quite thirsty work because I have to refill the birds' water bowl each morning. Sometimes, in their enthusiasm to empty the worm dish, even the water bowl is turned upside down.

In between feasting on the free meals I provide for them, the hedgehogs snout their way through the regularly hoed soil of the rose garden in search of juicy worms, grubs and slugs. Even above the voices of conversation and the television, we can hear these creatures of the night as they crunch their way through the peanut shells. They crouch low to the ground as they eat. Their spines lie flat, in an undefensive position, across their backs. Their perfectly shaped, rounded ears twitch from time to time and their bright eyes twinkle in the light. Their heads and snouts are covered with soft grey-brown hair, which from the neck to the back legs is longer and thicker, forming a hovercraft-like skirt.

If one of the hedgehogs does feel disturbed by the light or being watched, it will sometimes just sit still for a while, with its head lying sideways on the ground, watching with one eye and contemplating its next move.

The owl sometimes watches the hedgehogs from its lofty perch in the oak, or just in passing as it flies through the night on silent wings, in search of prey, to still its own hunger.

Farewell to April

As April nears its end it has presented us with warm, sunny days. Sunshine and soft rains have had a tremendous effect on the garden. The gentle hints of green on bushes, trees and shrubs are getting more pronounced and denser by the day. Spring really has arrived now, and with the first show of daisies came the mowing of the lawns. Gardening is so much more pleasant when the weather is favourable.

The daffodils have been a splendid sight. There has been a predominantly yellow profusion in all the neighbouring gardens, too, not only daffodil yellow but also that of the ever popular forsythia bushes.

The woodpeckers are chasing one another and the collared doves are still mating. On the whole, though, it seems the bird world has settled down to two by two. The courting days have gone, but not all were unscathed. High-speed chases through bushes and prickly holly were bound to leave their mark. One of the robins' right wing feathers is sticking out like an old-fashioned car indicator – Winger, however, does not seem too bothered by this.

One of the starlings, too, has more than its fair share of ruffled, displaced, untidy feathers. The cut-up dry pampas leaves have all disappeared and been put to good use, and the fluff from the tumble dryer is still eagerly gathered as soon as it is put out.

Although a little later this year, spring seems to be going hand in hand with nature to produce some spectacular sights and colour schemes. Many more colours on nature's palette are already being mixed, promising to meld into splendid hues in the coming months.

Memorable May Day

Any first of the month is much like the next. The first of this month, however, I have etched on my mind. I woke up to the call of my first cuckoo of the year and the first of the magnolia blossoms was out. I would dearly have loved to add another first, by the way of a photograph of the great spotted woodpecker. Although it was out in the garden all day, the camera-shy bird remained as elusive as a butterfly. To say nothing of the scarlet pimpernel: it, too, can be quite difficult to pinpoint as its flowers close in mid-afternoon, and especially if the weather is wet or dull.

The birds seem to have calmed down for the present since they have paired off, mated or are destined to remain unattached for this year, whichever the case may be. At feeding time, of course, the birds number as many as ever, but their activities don't seem quite as frantic as in the past few weeks.

The hedgehogs are as fascinating as before, from the point of view of there being a male, a female and an offspring, the three having hibernated and come through the harsh winter. Three of a kind, and yet they have distinctive and preferred tastes. Nothing has changed as regards to their eating habits: Spiky goes for the peanuts, Hedgy for the bread and very occasionally a piece of meat, while Prickles goes straight for the raw or cooked meats and fat.

Needless to say, putting out scraps of meat for Prickles also attracts the local cats. They are devious creatures and bide their time on the bottom lawn, amongst the rockery or the shrubs until they think that it is safe for them to rob the hedgehogs of their supper. Little do these felines know that I am as patient as they are, knowing full well that they will, as soon as they deem it safe to approach, try to make the most of a tasty meal of scraps. But not while I'm around!

The Delights of Spring

The month continues to be a sheer joy. Every day something new appears, shoots up and pushes through the soil or bark. All the varying shades of fresh green, from the lightest to the darkest, are blending with many other colours of spring, into a beautiful tapestry. Although the oak and some of the other deciduous trees are still waiting for their new dress, the garden looks an artist's paradise.

There is a new feature on the top lawn. I have lifted the turf and dug up the corner between the patio and the path on the right, and planted some slow-growing conifers and alpines. In this small area alone there are 12 different shades of green.

The turfs I have stacked into a grass wall along the path. During the lifting, digging, planting and stacking process, I unearthed what seemed like hundreds of worms. After every ten or so turns of the spade, I sat on the side patio for a few minutes, giving the waiting, hungry birds the opportunity to gather the wriggly, bonus pickings. The grass wall is now constantly being using as a landing strip by the birds and as a picnic site for the squirrels.

I had hoped to burn the stack of wood and brambles in the dell before there is the possibility of scorching new leaves. However, this will have to be a job for late summer or autumn because the pile has become a tower block of birds' flats. Wren, robin and blackbird couples were quick to seize the opportunity to make their homes in the stack.

One or two out of each bird species seem to be troubled with weight problems this year. Tubby, Chubby and Podgy apart, there are a couple of sparrows too which are rounder and fuller than the rest. A nuthatch has also joined the heavy brigade. Other than its distinctive colouring it would be quite unrecognisable because of its present rotund shape.

My ambition to capture Woody on celluloid is becoming quite an obsession. He remains shy and aloof and manages to keep a good distance between the camera and himself, and always catches me off-guard, when I least expect him, or the camera is out of reach.

The leaf buds of the great oak are noticeably swollen and lend a golden tan to the overall garden picture. Below, the daffodils still look as fresh as daisies and the azaleas are in flower. High above, the first swallows are tracing flight patterns across the changing skies, while down here the garden birds' throats are filled with rich and sonorous songs.

The 'Love Tree'

Well, it's all happening at once. The garden has taken on a wonderful fresh look. Within the last week, the oak's golden tan buds have burst open and out of their protective covering, young leaves have emerged.

The network of twigs and branches of other trees and bushes is densening with growing leaves. The dell is a mass of colours from buttercups, daisies, dandelions, deadnettles, violets, cuckoo pint, ferns and forget-me-nots, and there is a slight tint from the first of the bluebells.

The resident doves are still mating and only in the last few days has there been any sort of attempt at gathering nest material. When DJ and his betrothed fly into the garden, they are quickly shown the way out by Cooer, who strongly objects to their presence. Cooer and Dovey have quite taken over the garden, and for that matter, the bird table too.

Last year, when Tatty and Scruffy descended onto the patio, all the other birds – apart from a few cheeky sparrows – would fly off until the coast was clear again. Not so with their offspring. Cooer sees them off too and the magpies have to be quick and alert to pick up a few titbits while the dominant dove isn't looking.

The mistle thrushes seem to have abandoned their nest and flown elsewhere. Perhaps the interest the magpies and doves showed in the nest site was a warning to the thrushes and so they opted to build another nest away from the inquisitive birds.

On the 7th of May, I watched the squirrels for several hours. The three of them had a quick game of 'Catch Me If You Can' along the branches of the oak, and up and down and round and round the trunk. Eventually, Skipper went off, leaving Springer and Scamper in a relatively good-natured harmony. The two of them became inseparable. They followed each other around at a much more leisurely pace compared to the previous mad chases. They even sat on the door ledge together, eating nuts. Then they hopped across the lawn, past the herb patch, under the fence and up into the holly tree, just behind the fence in the garden next door.

They spent a good hour in the tree. Scamper watching Springer's every move, following her step for step, sniffing where she had sat, sitting for a moment where she had left a patch of warmth from her body. They only had time and eyes for each other, oblivious to the mating of a couple of sparrows and blackbirds just a branch or two away. At times they completely disappeared amid the prickly foliage of the holly. Perhaps it was during one of these moments that I missed the final act of their courtship, but I am sure that the youngsters found their adulthood in that love tree.

A little later. Scamper went off in the direction of his drey. Springer, with slow, deliberate hops, crossed the lawn again and climbed the oak. She ran along two, three branches, stopping every couple of feet, looking, sniffing as though she had lost something. Then she chewed off a few small twigs, bit off a couple of fresh shoots and promptly let the twigs fall to the ground, watching as they whirled down as if she was calculating how long it would take them to land on the lawn. This curious behaviour over. Springer clambered into the big box and lay there for a good half an hour. Then she climbed down to help herself to more nuts, eating her fill, burying some, before she too went off to settle down for the night.

Romantic Interlude

Watching the hedgehogs has become a regular ritual. In an earlier chapter I mentioned the difference in their size. Spiky, by far the biggest and exerting a certain amount of authority amongst the trio, I assume is either the mother or father of Hedgy and Prickles.

These two, having studied them a little closer now, are really more or less the same size, with Hedgy having just a slight advantage over Prickles who seems to have injured her snout somehow. It looks like a clown's plastic nose which has slipped to one side.

Spiky had come early and eaten some nuts before disappearing round the side of the house. Enter Prickles. It was almost as though Spiky had gone to fetch her and told her, 'Go on, it's your turn.' Prickles made straight for the dish of meat without hesitation.

A few minutes later, along came Hedgy. He kept walking around the dish and Prickles, trying every now and then to nudge his snout under her body, and finally making a clumsy attempt to get on her back. Until then I had no idea of the sex of either of them. But then that, I suppose, only matters to another hedgehog. Prickles refused to be disturbed by Hedgy's amorous advances. She certainly wasn't going to have her supper spoilt!

Hedgy tried again and again, to no avail. His frustration grew, and having been given the brush-off, he scuttled off across the lawn and out of sight. Shortly afterwards. Prickles followed his scent by taking the same zigzag route in pursuit. Somehow, they missed each other and soon Hedgy was back on the patio. He was bewildered. Where was Prickles? He ran this way and that, checking the dishes in passing, smelling, trying to pick up Prickles' scent.

At last she came back to the patio, wondering what all the fuss was about. For a moment she and Hedgy faced each other, snout against snout. That is when I retired to bed and your guess is as good as mine as to what, if anything, developed that night.

Five nights later. Spiky as usual was first on the patio and negating all I have said before: he decided to have some meat, for a change. Prickles joined him and dared to put her snout in the dish. Spiky vehemently objected to this and a scuffle broke out, with Prickles getting pushed and rolled about. Hedgy emerged out of the darkness and received the same treatment. Poor thing! He wasn't even anywhere near the dish when Spiky attacked.

I watched them coming and going, their scuffles, fights and feeding, until almost midnight, all the time sitting in the dark, watching over a little dish of meat, guarding it for the hedgehogs, making sure that the cats didn't cash in on a free meal.

Starlings in the Box

The weather has been quite kind recently, especially for gardeners. The changing temperaments of spring are varied. Today started off quite promising. The squirrels were up and about quite early, including Sally whom I was so pleased to see again after all this time. It was very friendly out there, in the oak and on the lawn, fence and patio. Quite a family atmosphere. At about nine o'clock Sally, Skipper and Scamper took their leave and left the run of the garden to Springer.

Then Woody swooped a steep, vertical descent from the oak onto the table and back into the oak, pecking vigorously at a few branches, sending dislodged pieces of bark flying to the ground. I sat and waited for Woody to come close enough again, for me to take his photograph. No such luck!

I did the washing instead. I hadn't quite finished pegging out the clothes when I felt a few drops of rain which soon turned into a deluge.

Swiftly, all the birds sheltered under bushes, amongst foliage, under and in the various boxes. About ten starlings gathered in a big box, one after the other, once the first two had found it to be the only dry place. They quickly called to the others and didn't hesitate to join them. Wet tails hung out over the entrance. Birds shook themselves inside the box, spraying each other with unwanted rainwater. It was a gathering of wet plumage and the starlings chattered, twittered and clicked noisily. Those already enjoying parenthood, and within sight or sound of their nests emitted loud whistles, 'Won't be long, just sheltering from the rain.'

The massive cloud which had hung over the garden broke up slightly, parts of it moving on. Weakened in its menacing strength, the deluge turned to heavy rain which soon gave way to a fine drizzle.

One starling, then two, six, ten, 20, descended onto the lawn and patio amid a large flock of other birds. Fresh notes trilled and chirped as the grass was being explored. The rain had brought the worms nearer to the surface, providing rich pickings for the birds.

Beaks were eagerly filled. Parents held juicy wrigglers tightly, letting them dangle down on either side. These, together with wet currants and soggy bread, were quickly flown to various nests and waiting hungry chicks, with their ever wide open, pink gapes.

May Dance

It was barely twilight when the first few bats flitted through the still air last night. And the night was but a few minutes old when I sighted the first hedgehog emerge from under the big holly tree. On straight legs it walked briskly along the path, behind the oak, past the rhododendron on its left, then the big boulder framed by the flame-coloured azalea to the right, and to the edge of the herb patch. Here it took a slight diversion onto the top part of the lower lawn towards the 'love tree'. Seconds later it was back on the path heading towards the patio. However, it scuttled straight on amongst the flower pots to the side of the house, out of sight.

Already I could see a second hedgehog which had come from the direction of the 'love tree'. Halfway along the same path it, too, diverted into the shrubbery, for several minutes only to emerge again with very definite intentions. It headed for the middle of the patio, sniffed the peanuts which I had already put out and dashed about in an undecided manner, or so it seemed.

By now I realised that the little explorer was none other than Prickles. She ran around the nuts. The little meat dish was by the side of one of the flower tubs. Prickles sniffed at it. Nothing. Just rainwater. Back to the nuts. Then the water bowl, which incidentally is the same colour as the meat dish, only bigger. Prickles knew exactly what she wanted. Sniff, sniff, and snort. 'What? No meat? Rainwater?!' And on to the water bowl.

'What's this? Tap water?'

I could almost read her thoughts. I opened a tin of meat in readiness for my sons' sandwiches and cut off a generous slice and cubed it to put into the meat dish. I had to wait almost a quarter of an hour before further action took place. Prickles returned, hotly pursued by Spiky.

129

Forget what I said about Spiky perhaps being the mother! Or the father! Well, in that case there is incest or else some other queer goings-on in the hedgehog world. Prickles had only just got to the dish containing the cubes of chopped ham and pork when suddenly there was Spiky, right at her side.

The dancing started immediately. Spiky walked around Prickles, first one way then the other, two, three laps at a time. Round and round. About turn and round and round again. Spiky was doing all the running, while Prickles almost pivoted on her back legs. Nose to nose and eye to eye, with Spiky not giving up the chase.

Hedgy came to within a few feet of the courting couple. He watched for a few minutes, at a distance. He had practised a short version of this same routine with Prickles only a few nights ago. Discretion being the better part of valour, Hedgy discreetly disappeared.

Some of the circles were tight, others wider. In the centre, Prickles moved, always backing away from Spiky, making sure that no more than her head, neck and shoulders were within Spiky's reach or smell. This dance routine continued in this manner for well over an hour. I am not sure whether they were doing the waltz, quickstep or just a plain ring-a-ring-a-hedgehog. Whatever Spiky's intention, Prickles was not ready for the prickly, amorous advances or suggestion of her suitor.

Much scuffling, sniffing and superb movements, by both male and female, ensued. Spiky circled Prickles two or three times one way and then changed direction. This ritual seemed to have a definite pattern to it, best known to hedgehogs. They were like a couple of pugilists, as most of the action was confined to one of the flagstones, as though it were a boxing ring. Even with the patio door closed and the TV on, I could hear their claws scraping the concrete. Could this be nothing more than a crude pedicure?

The dancing continued. In their eagerness to conquer and defend, the circles got bigger. Now the two of them had stepped out of their 'ring' to the adjoining flagstone. Twice, three times, they both missed their footing and rolled the 3 inches or so off the flag onto the lawn. Each time they were quick to regain a solid base and the waltzing continued. All the time Prickles kept her head turned sideways, keeping her injured snout out of the way for fear of being hurt even more.

Suddenly Spiky dashed off across the patio towards the rose garden. Did he have a call of nature? This seems to be as good an explanation as any for his swift disappearance and apparent disinterest in continuing the exhausting dance, for he was back as quickly as he had gone.

Prickles sat next to the meat dish. She stiffened slightly on Spiky's return. He though, ignored her completely and sat amongst the peanuts. Eagerly he crunched their shells to extract the nuts while Prickles, no more than a foot away, munched some of the cubes of meat.

Their stomachs taken care of. Spiky directed a few snuffs and snorts towards Prickles. To the night music of a cow mooing somewhere in the distance, a hooting owl, other sounds only audible to them, and the lapping, gurgling stream, they began to dance again. Their routine, by now, was both perfect and well rehearsed.

Then Prickles took a few steps backwards towards the door. Just a couple more steps. That was it. She pushed her backside firmly against the bricks below the door frame. Obviously a new routine, one with which Spiky couldn't come to terms. He pranced from side to side. No longer could he get anywhere near Prickles' rear. Climbing over her was obviously out of the question. So, the sideways movements continued with Prickles moving her front feet a few steps to the left, then to the right, depending on Spiky's intentions. He seemed to be getting quite agitated and he snorted vigorously. This wasn't fair! Prickles was making it very difficult for him.

Eventually the little lady took a couple of steps too many and she was forced away from the safety of the bricks, and round and round they spun again. They moved away, left towards the rose bed, and finally out of sight, blending with the dark earth.

Love, it seems, among the lower animals is a very complex, long-drawn-out affair, and certainly not a bed of roses where hedgehogs are concerned.

Newcomers

The garden, I am pleased to say, continues to flourish. Alas, the daffodils are not lasting quite as long as I had expected them to. I think this is mainly due to the torrential downpours we have had, which have also affected the tulips. But, as nature has it, as the petals of one species wilt and fall, so they are quickly replaced by other blooms, just as splendid or even more beautiful, in magnificent shades of colour.

The hatching of more and more chicks means that the business of collecting food from the patio is a keen affair by the various parents. The sparrows have learned a lesson from Woody, the tits and finches and have taken to the peanut bags like ducks to water. Since these pert chirpers have acquired their newly found skills, the bags need changing and or replenishing more often than just once a week as before.

Anything, it seems, goes in this garden and after many hours of observations it appears that a number of nature books will have to be rewritten or PS's added to their text as regards the habits and diets of birds and small wildlife.

Spring has claimed yet more casualties. Cooer's mate is limping badly. Two of her toes are very close together. She is obviously in some discomfort, and when she walks about, she places her left heel down first with her toes almost touching her breast. Cooer and Dovy, I just cannot make out. We are now in the last week of May and still these two are mating virtually every day. Yet, any nest-building activities are nothing more than very feeble attempts.

The 25th wasn't just a memorable day for the starving people of Africa, for whom the world sang; it was also a day to mark on the calender, as far as my garden is concerned.

I called Springer and Scamper as I put out more nuts. Usually they rush to the patio as soon as I call. But this morning – nothing! I watched the squirrels for about two hours before I realised that neither was Springer or Scamper, but two new babies. I expect that they are Sally's offspring. Had Sally brought her youngsters along to introduce them to the garden?

Sonny is a little smaller than Skelter. Between them they explored every blade of grass, the oak from the top to bottom, every slat of the left fence, even managing to get from one side to the other, between the gaps. The rose bushes, the rockery, wheelbarrow and tubs came under close scrutiny and they even tried to climb the steel washing line pole.

Although there wasn't an adult about, the little ones seemed to be clued up about the garden. They carefully followed the scents of their parents, brothers, sisters and cousins, taking time to familiarise themselves with all the smells.

Their exploration continued on Sunday and Monday, scrabbling up the trunk of the oak, playing in the big box, weaving their way back down, round and round the trunk, as though they were on a helter-skelter.

They played amongst the daffodil leaves and even nibbled a couple. They had play fights and miniature wrestling matches, and Sonny clung to Skelter's back, hitching a ride, a number of times. Perhaps Sonny already realised that he is different from his sister, and is practising his male instincts ready for next spring.

The small box held some kind of fascination for both the youngsters. They climbed in and their sparring continued, while taking turns in looking out or sitting on the platform. Then the head of the other would appear. There seemed to be heads and tails everywhere and at times it was hard to believe that there were only two young squirrels in the box. Also, at times it looked as though their playful antics would make them lose their footing and send them both crashing through the oak branches to the ground below, especially when they ventured along thin twigs to the very tips, to chew off new, succulent growth. Each time these young twigs bent and threatened to snap under the extra weight.

Fortunately, luck and the good Lord were on their side, and the little ones had come to no harm by the time they hopped off to their drey for a rest, early in the afternoon.

Prickles in My Hands

I had never seen hedgehogs close to, until Spiky, Hedgy and Prickles started paying regular nightly visits. Without the food supply, watching their activities might well have been impossible.

Prickles was the only one I saw on Sunday evening. She was on the lawn near the oak at dusk and I quickly put out some meat scraps. I wanted to change the water too, as a couple of starlings had earlier taken their evening bath in it. Just as I got to the door with the jug, Prickles was already sitting under the ledge. Not to frighten her, the water would have to wait.

I knelt down with my head bent low to just above the spiny body. I put on my gardening gloves and gently picked Prickles up. Instinctively she curled up. With this little ball cupped in both hands I sat in the lounge. After a couple of minutes of talking to her, she uncurled, obviously realising that she was in no danger.

I was able to see her lovely soft face, her bright, beady eyes and her damaged snout. This seems to have healed quite well and doesn't look as angry and sore as it did when I first noticed the injury some weeks ago.

After about ten minutes of getting acquainted with each other, I set Prickles down on the patio. I removed my gloves and she allowed me to stroke her for several minutes more before I said goodnight to her. She ran to the edge of the patio when she remembered her supper, turned, and spent half an hour or so eating the meat scraps.

This new experience we shared is certainly something for me to write about, and who knows, Prickles might deem it important enough for her to tell her grandchildren about coming face to face with me.

Sandy

Skipper has been keeping himself to himself lately. However, somewhere amongst the trees along the stream or the nearby woodland he has found a young lady squirrel. Sandy, the female in question, is slim, dove-grey, with petite features and a lovely tail with every hair on it in its proper place.

They arrived together on Monday morning. Skipper allowed Sandy a little time to get used to the new surroundings and even told her where the nuts are kept. Cautiously she approached the patio, skirted the tub of pansies, clambered behind it onto the flower pot full of stones, and hesitantly knocked a nut off the ledge. She raced halfway towards the oak, sat on her haunches and noisily devoured the nuts. She was only allowed to fetch two more nuts before Skipper had other ideas.

For more than two and a half hours he followed her about. I don't think there is much of the oak they didn't cover. Skipper always in pursuit, stopping briefly, sniffing, smelling, getting close to Sandy, before she again lengthened the gap between them.

In all that time they rested three times, sitting quite still on the same bough or the fence with no more than 12 slats between them. Occasionally Sandy remembered the nuts and hopped over to the patio. Twice, Skipper went frantic, running along the fence, down to the base, back up, leaping to a nearby tree, tearing across the rose bed and lawn and up into the oak along half a dozen branches in frenzied search of Sandy.

When finally he spotted her, he hotly pursued her again until they eventually went off together, presumably to a love nest or somewhere private in one of the trees upstream. After some 15 to 20 minutes, Skipper returned alone. His pace was leisurely as he hopped across the lawn. He climbed the left fence and from there ambled his way through familiar branches leading him downstream and home.

Not long after, Sandy reappeared, and for a little while the garden, oak and patio belonged to her and the birds. Until, that is, Springer, Scamper and the youngsters reclaimed everything. Perhaps we have two expectant mums now. It seems to me that being in love is as exhausting for squirrels as it is for hedgehogs.

Baby Minder

So much has been happening over the last few days that I can hardly write fast enough to keep up with what's been going on.

There aren't two but three new baby squirrels. When I first saw number three, it was busy stripping some bark off one of the smaller oak branches. Stripper joins in the play and the sheer joy of spring and the newness of it all.

It seems that Stripper is a bit of a tomboy. My friend who made the bird table said, knowing all about the squirrels, 'I've made the table leg in steel, so that the squirrels can't climb up!' That worked fine until Stripper came along. Like a true trapeze artist he shins up the pole, reaches for the nut bag, hangs onto it and pulls the nuts out, which he eats, hanging upside down. Sometimes he'll climb onto the table and lowers himself down the bag.

The next squirrel came along to do the same and pulled the bag so far over that the little one could sit on the fence while holding onto the bag. As he was eagerly chewing through the net to be able to get at the nuts a bit easier, they dropped out underneath. They rained down the fence amongst the rose bushes where tits and finches were quick to pick up the kernels.

Play-fighting, leaping, jumping and balancing is all being practised by the trio. They still have a lot to learn. They already know that there are nuts to be found on the door ledge. Sally now puts in brief appearances from time to time but it seems that Springer has been appointed as chief governess. She is very tolerant with the youngsters and lets them get quite close to her, provided she doesn't happen to have a nut in her mouth at the time.

Songs of May

Yesterday, I started recording the beautiful songs of May. This morning one of the rooks was making such a din that it woke me up and kept me awake. By six o'clock I was up and recording again.

Within minutes of each other Springer, Sonny, Skelter and Stripper arrived. They played catch and had early morning bouts of all-in wrestling.

At a quarter past seven, the first of the starling babies was introduced to the patio. The 'love tree' was absolutely alive with sparrows, blackbirds, starlings and their young. The chirps and squawks of the adults were drowned by the ever-hungry calls of the young. Bird seed, cooked rice, bread and currants disappeared at an unbelievable rate. Each time every crumb had been pecked up, the 'Please can we have some more?' begging calls came to a fever pitch.

It was a long and busy day for me and the garden residents. I felt that they were keeping me company all day to make up for the lost time because I had been working for ten out of the past 14 days.

I felt rewarded by the presence of all my little friends, as indeed I rewarded them in turn. A small price indeed, for the pleasure of watching them and the delight of their perpetual songs.

A Week Away

As the 31st of May approached and the thought of a week away from it all began to sink in, I felt less and less like spending seven days away from my garden.

The Tenby Golf Club Open Week, as always, was a roaring success. While my husband played golf every day, I spent my time visiting my family, former neighbours, and looking up friends. It was lovely to see them all again and to catch up with all the news. Proudly I showed off photographs of my 'living garden', of birds, squirrels, hedgehogs, flowers, plants and trees.

Our chalet was very comfortable and backed onto woodland. Just a few feet away from the back windows stood aged hazel, holly, oaks and whitethorn, home to sparrows, robins, bullfinches, collared doves and wood pigeons.

From this wooded ridge the ground fell away steeply for some 30 to 40 feet to a boggy gully, which in winter or after persistent rainfall is probably quite a little stream. From there the ground rose gently, leaving ferns, red campion, bluebells, wood anemones and bird's nest ferns behind, and rose further, amongst century-old pine trunks which stood erect and tall, reaching hundreds of feet above their roots to their swaying, green crowns.

The ancient sun has long threaded its rays through these very branches, to play amongst the tall trunks right down to ground level, to tease the woodland floor. Although this could now be likened to modern laser beams, it is still the old sun which plays and teases, which lets birds, in flight, penetrate its rays, and allows insects to ride on its colourful beams. This natural beauty was almost like home from home – but not quite.

Throughout the week, I put up a brave front. My thoughts

were back home in the garden. I had been homesick for West Wales after we first moved. Now the tables were turned.

Home Again

Despite some weeds, and the lawns crying out to be cut, the garden looked welcoming on our return. It seemed greener and even denser than a week ago, almost as if everything had been trying to catch up with, and surpass, spring. I had Saturday afternoon to myself and I was able to absorb my beautiful surroundings at leisure.

Prickles and Hedgy came that evening and munched the meat scraps and peanuts. As the last notes of a male blackbird's beautiful song melted with the darkness, I put food out for those who would be taking part in the dawn chorus.

The sun shone warm the next morning and the breeze was tepid. By the time the birds were on their third breakfast, I had counted 15 young starlings. The sparrow chicks numbered even more.

Three baby blackbirds are already independent. They still have that beautiful warm brown colouring, but even at this tender age two of them are sporting glossy black tails and wing feathers, just like their father.

Other blackbird parents still have nestlings which they are feeding at frequent intervals. The little sparrows are as cunning as ever. They chirp loudly, wings fluttering furiously and beaks wide open, waiting to be fed. But when Mum and Dad aren't looking, the babies manage to feed themselves quite well.

So, too, it is with the starlings. A few of the young are more advanced and feed themselves and are already looking more like the slim adults as opposed to the rounded, fluffy younger birds. Some of these are trying to feed themselves too. As they pick up pieces of bread or currants, with their beaks open wide, just as though they were being fed, they still lack the coordination of closing their upper and lower mandibles in order to secure a mouthful of food.

One of these little chaps has a terrible cold. He coughs and sneezed quite a lot and sounds more like a frog than a hungry baby starling.

After a marked absence of the resident robins for well over three weeks, I was pleased to see them back. I had never noticed them going missing for such a long spell before. If anything, robins are generally loyal to their gardens and environment. How far, and wherever it was that they went, I am so glad to see them home again.

There are Friends and There are Friends

I watched the life in the garden for several hours on Sunday morning before I reluctantly decided to wash the holiday laundry.

Sonny, Skelter and Stripper delighted me with their tumbling, rolling, jumping and wrestling. Scamper and Sandy were there too, taking respectful turns in getting nuts from the ledge and the bowl inside. Stripper performed his party trick and deftly hoisted himself up the table leg.

It was late afternoon when I mowed and raked the lawns, hoed the rose bed and swept the paths and patios. I noticed many buds on the rose bushes, and the rockery looks quite healthy, despite its position, with fresh sprigs of new growth on the heathers. The pink rhododendron, which I had transplanted from the bank behind the big holly, has for the first time two beautiful, dark red blooms, with the promise of more buds to flower.

Yesterday morning I worked and returned just in time to see Stripper climbing up the bird table leg. It had been damp all night and even as I watched the little acrobat, it was drizzling. Stripper managed to push and pull himself up to level of the top of the peanut bag. Before the little squirrel could decide whether to climb onto the table or free his front legs to reach for the bag, he slowly began to slide down the smooth, wet pole. The expression on his face was absolutely priceless as he slipped down, down, down, while he kept his eyes firmly fixed on the overhanging, disappearing, out of reach, peanuts. From ground level, his nostrils eagerly received the scent of the wet nuts.

Further attempts to conquer the slippery pole failed several times more. Then, this fast-learning youngster had to agree that the nuts, in their shells, on the ledge of the door, were much easier to get at. Life had taught Stripper yet another valuable lesson.

Well, the squirrels, birds and hedgehogs know that I am back. I think the garden does too. For my part, I am so glad to be home again with all my little friends.

Italian Cuisine

Stripper played 'house'. He tore along the oak branches, chewing off small twigs with leaves and rushed to the big box with them, arranging them carefully in the left corner, before dashing off again to nip off another twig.

I had watched Stripper's grandfather perform the same ritual. In his eagerness to amass the twigs in the corner of the box, Sam always managed to sweep the last twig out with his tail while arranging the next one. Stripper was much more careful about the whole thing.

After our evening meal I had put out some cooked spaghetti. Normally, such leftovers I cut up into beak-size pieces for the birds. I had been in a bit of a rush and needed the bowl, so I just tipped the strings of pasta out into a messy heap.

Just as darkness was about to take over from dusk, Prickles came running along the path from the bottom lawn. Without standing on ceremony, she tucked into the spaghetti like a true Italian. After a quarter of an hour of gorging herself she dissolved into darkness, near the oak, to make way for Spiky. He, too, enjoyed the variation of the menu.

The next morning, the little of the pasta which had been left was soon polished off by eager beaks with ever-open gapes.

Later, Skelter, Sonny and Stripper played 'house' together. They had a sort of party where each one had to bring something. Skelter took a leafy twig and patted it down amongst those already there. Shortly afterwards Sonny joined her, bearing his contributions. The party was already in full swing when Stripper jumped onto the top of the box from an overhead bough and looked in, over the edge. I doubt if he could see much through the arrangement of leaves blocking his vision. 'Room for one more?' and the trio romped about in the box for quite some time, thoroughly enjoying their little world and life.

Squirrels-in-Waiting

Scamper, from ground level, had watched the goings-on of the youngsters but he had no time for such frivolous nonsense. He collected nuts, two at a time, and leaped across the lawns in great bounds and disappeared for about ten minutes. This exercise was repeated a number of times before he finally succumbed to his own hunger.

Scamper's determined efforts to carry nuts from A to B seems to suggest that Springer is confined to the drey. I have not seen her since before we left for Tenby. The timing would be about right, in which case I hope that all will go well. If my assumption is correct then little Scamper has turned into a wonderfully caring, considerate husband.

Just before lunch, a jay paid a flying visit. The bird is handsomely covered with pinkish-brown plumage, with a black and white streaked head and wing feathers which also sport a bright blue patch at the top of the wings. His black tail feathers and white rump seem to match his other end by way of a white throat edged by a black walrus-type moustache either side from his beak to his throat. He looks as though he has been assembled from lots of leftover feathers – on a Friday afternoon! But for all that, he looks quite beautiful.

Jay sat in the oak, watching countless birds feeding on the patio and the squirrels playing on the lawn. For a minute I thought that the bird would join in the feasting, but his shyness got the better of him and moments later he flew off.

The jay I had seen last year was quite small and must have been a young one, judging by the size of today's visitor.

I do hope that Jay will call again, often. Perhaps his visit, short though it was, was a good omen for Springer and Scamper and their expected happy event.

New Home

When I start work at six o'clock in the morning, I get up at about half past four. This gives me plenty of time to shower, dress, feed my feathered friends and furry animals, and enjoy their soothing company.

How delightful these early mornings are. I wonder how many people are able to appreciate such delights or, indeed, are aware of them. I do miss the garden terribly on these full working days and it makes it such a pleasure to return to.

For about a week now the three youngsters have been having a great time in the oak, at least from their point of view. They have nibbled off umpteen little twigs, which they have promptly let drop. The discarded foliage lies strewn over a wide area beneath the oak. Three times I have raked this mess up and still the lawn is being covered with bits of oak. Until yesterday, that is.

When I returned after a nine and a half hour working day, Stripper, Skelter and Sonny were tumbling about around the base of the oak. The three of them get on great together and seem to be wonderful friends and playmates.

Although there were still some nuts on the ledge I put some more out and called over to the young squirrels, just to let them know that I was back. Stripper came bounding across the lawn straight away. Skelter stayed where she was with a nut she had just unearthed, and Sonny scrabbled up the oak with tremendous agility and showered a few more oak sprigs onto the lawn.

Some days ago I had already noticed that quite a lot of these twigs and leaves, instead of twirling to the ground, had lodged in a fork, high up in the oak. At the time and, once or twice since, I thought that it had all the makings of a drey.

Yesterday evening the activities of nipping off small twigs was stepped up for a while, with two of the squirrels disappearing with yet another twig, amongst the foliage in the fork. The job in hand was completed by eight o'clock and shortly afterwards I saw two of the squirrels nose their way into the drey and settle down for the night. It is likely that all three of them spent the night in this newly constructed abode. If they did, then the third one sneaked in while I wasn't looking.

One, two, three. It makes no difference. They are most welcome and I wish them well in their new home.

Victim

How can one day end on such a happy note as seeing new neighbours moving into the oak, and the next begin with tragedy?

I was having a well-earned lie-in this morning. I heard a dreadful commotion in the garden. I looked out of the window just in time to see the black and white, blue-collared tom with a baby starling in its mouth running along the fence.

Helpless, I saw the assassin disappear with its victim and the frightened squeaks for help from the baby could still be heard from about four gardens away. When the panic-stricken cries of the other birds subsided, the whole garden fell silent. Not a peep was heard for 15 minutes before a sparrow, tentatively, asked if everything was all right now.

Slowly, sadly, one by one the birds began to discuss the loss of one of their numbers, each telling the other to be more vigilant.

This could have been the start of a beautiful day. The sun was bright, the air warm and the sky is a perfect blue.

Alas! The laws of nature deal some cruel hands at times.

Ailing and Abetting

The baby starling with the bad cold became an outcast for a few days. He seemed to be eating well and drinking, too. But while his brothers and sisters were being fed and cared for by the parents, he was left to fend for himself, poor little chap.

Between beaksful of food and drink he seemed to be gasping for air most of the time. With a little sunshine on his back, I hope that he will soon get better. I don't particularly want to make a habit of becoming an undertaker for starlings.

I had never realised that birds can be prone to coughs and sneezes. Chickens, yes.

Last year while staying with friends in the south of Italy, I spent more than a week nursing one of their ailing pullets. She had had nothing to eat or drink for three days. The weather was scorching hot, even in the shade. I took the little hen under my 'wings' and many times during the day I carried her into the garage, filled my hand with water from the tap and offered the refreshing liquid to Hanna. It took several attempts before she realised that I meant well. Then she started to eat out of my hand, and for a number of days, I became her only source of food and drink. She and I had many a chat as Hanna sat on my lap or was cradled in my arm. While I stroked her and talked to her she replied with croaking, throaty clucks, almost as though she understood everything I said to her.

After about ten days of me beginning my role as mother hen, Hanna perked up. A few times she strutted over to where I was sitting on the patio. It had taken me a while to realise what it was she wanted me to do, as she walked towards me, clucking turning and walking off again, stopping, looking at me, clucking and coming back, clucking more insistently. I thought that she wanted water from the garage, and got up to go to where the bowls of feed and water were. She ran the last few feet and pecked eagerly at the corn and then greedily drank of the, by then, tepid water.

I got the message. This had been Hanna's way of showing me that she was better and could now feed herself again.

The little sick starling is much improved although I cannot claim to have had a hand in his recovery. Happily he is back in favour with the rest of the family, his conscience-stricken parents feeding him as though to make up for lost time.

I have noticed the other babies sneezing, too, every time they have taken a drink from the bowl. Perhaps they dip their beaks too far into the water and get liquid trapped in their lores or eyes which they can then only expel by sneezing. The adults tend to shake their heads after drinking. Maybe this is something the little ones have to learn.

Barring mishaps, the baby, well on the way to full recovery, will enjoy fatherhood this time next year and for years to come.

Sons and Daughters

Blackytu, son of Blacky and Sooty, has young ones in various locations in the garden, now that they have fledged. Like all my residents and visitors, whatever food happens to be on the patio for them, the blackbirds show a marked favour for currants.

Blackytu seems to be a single parent and has a full-time job feeding his youngsters. We have become quite close. He seems to know that I understand his problem of being a lone parent and has accepted that I am a constant supply of food for him and his.

Even when the currant supply is getting low outside, Blackytu is first in the queue for more. I sit on the door ledge and call him. He comes running, head down, along the path and across the lawn, and when he is only inches from me I drop a few currants which he pecks up eagerly. Then I tell him not to be greedy. 'That's enough. Go and feed your babies and then come back.'

Obediently, he does just that. With an empty beak he races back to me and the procedure is repeated. While talking and encouraging him, he replies with grateful clucks and continues to go about his business in hand – or should that be, beak!

Jay and Co.

A few days ago Jay spent quite some time in the garden. It was just as though he was seeing it for the first time. I positioned myself out of direct sight, with the camera, finger on the button. I waited and waited but Jay didn't come close enough for a good clear picture.

From nowhere and much to my surprise a baby pied woodpecker landed on the peanut bag, suspended above the door. I clicked, delighted with this unexpected bonus. At last, I had a record of a great spotted.

Several days later I woke to what seemed like a noisy convention of the bird world. My first thought was: cats! My rude awakening came from within the oak.

Downstairs, I parted the blinds slowly and just caught sight of Jay winging his way into the oak from the patio. His protests at being disturbed were loud, raspy croaks and screeches. When it felt safe, he descended onto the lawn again, looking about him for signs of danger and calling up to the oak. Jay's mate flew onto the table, also calling and coaxing.

Then, one by one their three offspring, guided by their parents, left the seclusion of the oak and flew: one on the washing line, one on the left fence and the third came to rest on the grass wall. The young, as handsome and as colourful as the parents, and already the size of the resident doves, joined in what seemed to be a heated discussion.

For no apparent reason. Jay and his mate took off, leaving their young behind. Was this their way of introducing the family to the garden?

Later that day the youngsters were still exploring their surroundings. Then each one selected a tree. One, the oak; another, the oak next door; and the third, the elm two gardens away. Their game of 'guess where I am' began. They exchanged notes of 'quick – quick', the loudest coming out of the big oak, an echoing, quieter call from three trees away.

Since that day the young jays have become quite a regular part of the life in the garden, and between them they add a spectacular array of colours. Their dusky pink upper bodies, white rumps, black tails and wing-tips with flashes of blue on their upper wings and their black 'Charlie Chan' moustaches stand out beautifully against the predominantly green backdrop of their surroundings.

The young jays have become very friendly with Stripper, Skelter and Sonny and share the oak in amicable harmony. Sometimes they play catch, hopping, jumping and flying from bough to branch, up and down, never putting too much distance between them.

I have also noticed a jay sitting no more than a couple of feet away from one of the squirrels on the same bough. Both were keen to show their preening skills to each other. They went through their individual cleaning processes in turn, almost as if one was trying to outdo the other.

This friendly interlude lasted some ten minutes when the squirrel played his trump card. Did he say to the jay, 'Watch me. I bet you can't do this!'

Squirrel hooked his back claws firmly into the bark and swung his body to and fro, as he hung upside down. The little jay didn't quite know what to make of this and took to his wings, directing a few sharp 'quick – quick', calls at the squirrel, from a neighbouring tree, as if to say, 'OK pal. You win.'

Bird Box to Let

No previous owner. Clean, well built and conveniently situated in much-sought-after area with all local amenities ... Such an advertisement could well have been taken out of a wildlife magazine produced by the wildlife themselves.

I had seen several wasps hovering around one of the nesting boxes on the right fence. Were these wasps scouts, looking for a new home?

A few days passed and the activities increased. The box, especially around the entrance, was a-buzz. The slight gap between the front wall and roof was quickly closed with grey layers of a quick-drying mass-produced waste. The layering continued and within a week the entrance too was caked over and filled in, bar a small opening which serves as entrance and exit. At first glance the grey mass looks just like a fungus one sometimes sees on old, withered trees.

Contracts have been signed and sealed. The wasps have moved in. The birds don't seem to mind. They sit on top of the box or the fence and chirp, not intending any offence towards the wasps, and none is taken.

My association with wasps, bees and hornets over the years, right back to my childhood, have certainly not been happy ones. However, if relationships continue on the apparently good wasps–birds basis, I will be quite happy to leave the wasps to their new home, provided that they in turn respect my presence in the garden and leave me alone.

Abroad and Home

The days and weeks passed quickly and the holiday preparations were in full swing with our departure date on the calender. Naturally the photographs of the garden and residents travelled with us and were viewed with much interest amid oohs and aahs from friends and relatives alike. We stayed in Hanover with dear friends who visited us last year. They listened eagerly to updates of the squirrels, birds and hedgehogs.

On a walk along the Maschsee, in Hanover, we watched ducks and swans and listened to the birds, their songs accompanying us along the paths through the shady woods.

On another beautiful day we travelled south along the west side of the Harz Mountains and then across some of its mountainous region, stopping a few times to take in the wild and wonderful scenery, filling our lungs with pure, pine-scented air. Our destination was Bad Harzburg, famous for its spa waters, rich in iron and minerals and healing, soothing properties. Unfortunately the baths were closed for the day.

A ride in a cable car compensated for the baths. We reached the first section high above ground level where once a castle had looked down upon the sleepy town. From there we walked some 3 kilometres up and across to the edge of the mountain and the welcome of the Rabenklippe restaurant. From the edge of this was a sheer drop of several hundred feet to the valley behind the mountain, thus separating it from the valley we left an hour ago.

Exploring the vantage points around us we saw several young, red squirrels, half the size of our youngsters back home. The reds seemed quite tame and very agile, to the point of clawing their way from a nearby pine up a perpendicular almost smooth rock face to the flower boxes on top of the veranda. From there, they took a short-cut along tables, benches and the terrace to the trees beyond, only casually stopping to look at the people.

En route back to Ostende we stopped off just 25 miles short of the Dutch border crossing at Venlo. There we stayed with some relatives of mine for a few days. My young niece and her husband and baby son live in a rented farmhouse, upstairs, while my nephew and his wife live downstairs. What used to be pigsties and barns they have cleverly and beautifully converted and renovated. The house is part of a large farm complex surrounded by widespread fields and woods.

On a long walk we were delighted to see red deer, pheasants, grouse, moorhens, rabbits and hares. The sky was black with tweeting and twittering, wheeling, whirling, diving and falling, circling swallows, while on the ground wood pigeons pecked what they could find lying about on the already harvested wheat fields. Across our path, between two sugar beet fields, hopped tiny toads. Grasshoppers chirped along the way and we could hear the lapping waters of the little brook just beyond the fields.

We arrived home on Saturday, thoroughly relaxed and still talking about our wonderful holiday to which relatives, friends and nature contributed so much joy.

Nature is quite beautiful, at home as well as abroad.

Two More Mouths to Feed

Prior to our holidays, I had left the garden mowed, hoed, weeded and brushed. In short, like a little park.

Now, the top lawn was littered with peanut shells and dried-up leafy twigs lay strewn below the oak. Some of the rose petals have dropped off too but on the whole the garden, birds and squirrels bade us a warm welcome.

Of our three sons, the two who were at home were in charge of feeding the birds and animals. A young nature lover, Nigel, son of friends of ours, was pleased to be asked to organise the lunchtime feeding. He coped admirable and took his task seriously. One or two squirrels even took peanuts out of his hands. This delighted the 11-year-old no end and I have my suspicions that he is quite sorry that we are back already.

On Saturday afternoon there were seven squirrels in the garden and the hectic business of collecting nuts from the ledge was quite a serious one. The youngsters have grown a little and are a fortnight older. The jays have filled out as well and flash through the garden in their attire of beautifully coloured plumage.

I forgot to put peanuts out on the patio for the hedgehogs on Sunday night. We heard Spiky arrive. So who needs peanuts on the patio? An intelligent, compromising hedgehog such as Spiky doesn't, after all, need to be spoon fed. He got up on his hind legs, and between snout and front paws managed to get the nuts off the ledge, all by himself, thank you very much!

Last night I left the nuts on the ledge on purpose, to see what would happen. As soon as we heard a scrabbling noise, my husband and I investigated It was pitch dark. The spiky shape was smaller than Spiky. More movement, and two tiny pin cushions joined the first. So. Prickles had done it! She had become a mother.

Well done! The little ones are still very young and no more than a handful between them.

I hope that their mum will tell them about the advantages of living in a garden where they are safe and don't have to cross any busy roads.

Courting Couple in August

I was on the verge of waking up. In my semi-conscious stupor, I heard a noise which shortly afterwards roused me out of my sleep oblivion. My watch pointed to 4 am. Realising what the noise was, I went to the window and opened it.

Below, on the patio, were two hedgehogs. For the next half an hour I watched a repetition of the May Dance, except that this was a much noisier love affair.

The bigger of the two did all the running around what was his centre of attraction. The female turned tight circles, her head always where she could see and keep an eye on her suitor. Throughout the wooing, she snorted continuously, sometimes even sounding angry. Her noisy objections towards the amorous male broke through the otherwise silent night.

How long this had been going on for, I could not say. Just as the cold was getting to me, the male dashed away to where the peanuts lay, leaving the female still snorting and snuffling, five flagstones away.

A moment later, she disappeared amongst the rose bushes, under the fence and into the next garden, still voicing her objections.

No doubt he would find her again before retiring for the day. If not this night, then the next or the one after would see their union blessed.

Broken Holidays

Many rivers have emptied their volumes into the seas since my last chapter.

Pressures and demands on my precious time have kept me out of my garden. All this was to be eased by a fortnight's holiday on a Greek island. Fate, however, had other plans and on the fifth day I met with an horrendous accident, the details of which I will spare you. It will suffice to say that it took six months of grit, guts and fight to be able to walk again, minus a zimmer or crutches. Inevitably, some bright sparks came up with helpful suggestions like, 'Put your best foot forward!'

I missed the garden terribly. From my bed in the dining room, I could see the squirrels scrabbling up and down the oak, and the birds on the table, and the peanut bag. For a few months of long and agonising nights I could hear the hedgehogs crunching their supper.

The months were endless and I looked forward to the spring and to be able to tend the garden and see all my little residents again.

I hoped that they, too, would sense that my absence would only be a temporary one rather than any deliberate neglect on my part.

Premature Flight

One of my bedroom windows looks down on the side of next door's house and most of their back garden. I noticed an unfamiliar bird on top of their shed. It was one I had never seen before. Obviously a juvenile, about the size of a blackbird. Its feathers were anything but sleek – just been blow-dried but not brushed down! Ruffled feathers but not arranged again. Tousled, but nothing a little more growing and preening wouldn't fix in time.

My neighbour came out with a saucer of food and placed it on top of the shed for the young bird. Either it didn't know what to do with it or it wasn't hungry. It walked back and forth along one side of the roof. Then it had little preening sessions before it was time for walkabout again. It looked over the edge of the side of the shed as though contemplating jumping on to the roof of my shed.

It stretched one of its wings as far as it would stretch and then flapped both wings before tucking them away quite neatly. And all this time a magpie flew back and forth, helping himself to whatever was on the sauce.

In the past I have spent many hours watching the goings-on in my garden. Now I didn't have time for this – gardening was on my agenda. I went downstairs and out through my side door to get around the back to the shed.

From the top of the lawn a magpie and a big black crow flew off, leaving behind a twitching bundle of grey feathers and soft down. Even as I looked and saw the last twitch, the squab's little breast heaved no more. I don't know whether it had been the young collared dove or a wood pigeon.

I went next door to tell my neighbour of the baby's passing.

She had found it by the side of her shed amongst some discarded pots and had put it on the shed roof, out of the way of her cats.

Minutes later, in my own back garden again, there was a trail of feathers along where the little body had been dragged and a crow had made a meal of it. The headless corpse was lying on its back, wings spread out, its chest cavity bloodied and devoid of organs and entrails.

I gathered up what little was left of the bird and donned my funeral director's hat, yet again. The squab's eagerness to take to its wings before they were strong enough had cost it its life.

Thieving Magpies and Jays

A song thrush had built her nest in one of next door's trees, covered from the bottom to three-quarters of the way to the top in thick ivy. Several storeys above her nest, a drey had been carefully constructed.

This became home to six offspring. I watched them as the squirrels tentatively ventured out, one by one. They stuck close together, sniffing, testing this branch and the next. Dashing here and there. Familiarising themselves with the smells of their elders.

The thrush's chicks had hatched. Although most elusive, she became quite agitated and very vocal when danger was about. The young magpies had fledged some time ago and were very aggressive en masse. They frequented the oak with their loud chatter. Their din was ear-splitting.

The thrush flapped and flitted from branch to bough, from here to there, doing her best to divert the attention of the magpies from her precious home. Her frantic calls sounded like a more subdued echo of the magpies' chatter.

Both magpies and jays are menacing predators of nestlings. I am no lover of cats, but they have had a pretty bad press over the years, being responsible for the deaths of thousands of birds every year. At least by the time they catch a bird off guard, the bundle of feathers will have had a taste of life already, as opposed to those which, as they fledge, get picked off by the jays and magpies.

Perhaps new strategies need to be adopted. Fly the nest when the big bullies aren't looking. Take care, little ones. Be on guard, always.

Two Firsts in One Night

It never ceases to amaze me. The more I watch, the more I learn. I had put some peanuts out, as usual, for the hedgehogs' supplementary night snack. Some nuts had fallen into the diamond-shaped cut-outs of my black rubber mat outside the patio door.

After some waiting the security light came on and one of the hedgehogs was there, eagerly chomping away at the nuts by the side of my mat. It then moved onto the mat. That is when I saw the hedgehog nose into a diamond, but fail to extract a nut. It sat back slightly and scooped the nut out with one of its front paws. I had never seen the paws put to good use like that before. I have seen hedgehogs stopping to have a scratch. I have seen males covering their backs with saliva – this apparently is like presenting their mate with a bunch of flowers or some sort of love token – but this clawing dexterity was something new.

The light went on and off as the last supper revellers frequented my outdoor restaurant. New additions for them were several cut-up milk cartons filled with water, to replace the saucers and dishes which were always getting upset and tipped up. I noticed one of my little visitors had done a belly flop into the carton, but still managed to quench its obvious thirst.

A little while later, after scurrying about across the top patio, sniffing and smelling as it did so, it suddenly stopped. It sort of lay on its left side, turned its head and licked the spines of the right side of the body. Well, I had never seen that before, either!

Songs of the Wren

On the side patio, in the corner between the lounge and sitting room windows, I had planted a pyracantha and a *Rudbeckia laciniata*. They have grown well and have merged together almost as one bush. I had fixed a small nest box in the depth and safety of the thorny pyracantha.

Once again Jenny-Wren had shown interest in the site, and flew about, surveying it from the fence opposite, from the stand of mixed firs and from the ivy-clad fence further down. Satisfied with her surroundings, she began to refurbish the interior of the box and turned it into a neat, comfortable home. She will have used grass, leaves, feathers, wool and moss for furnishings and finishing touches to raise her second brood of the season.

During the long winter, I had again saved the fluff from the filter of my tumble dryer and distributed bits of it here and there on bushes and branches, in case any birds might find it useful.

For several weeks the wren has delighted me with her beautiful melodious song. What a voice for one so little! More recently she has emerged twice, three times a day from within the box to sit on the farthest, outer tip of the branch of a nearby fir tree and has immediately recited her clear, sweet song, her jubilant trills penetrating throughout the garden.

These open-air recitals more than likely have served several purposes. They got the wren out of her enclosed environment to stretch her wings and legs and for some well-earned fresh air. Somewhere in the passage of her vibrant song, was probably a proclamation of imminent motherhood. Her ventures into the garden became less frequent as the all-important business of brooding began in earnest.

Soon, and both parents flitted back and forth quickly and

unobtrusively with small grubs, at first, then spiders, caterpillars and all sorts of insects and morsels for the tiny, ever-open gapes. I had been out almost all day on Tuesday. On Wednesday the traffic to and from the nest was one of constant rush hour. Another day out on Thursday.

Late afternoon, and the little brood was very verbal. Even through the closed window, I could hear the peeps of the chicks. On and on they seemed to call for their mother and food. I watched but saw no activity as before. I went out, to investigate in case one of the chicks had fallen out of the nest. All seemed OK. I parted a couple of twigs and saw two little heads peeking out of the box.

I noticed only the hen seeing to her chicks. Had he left her to fend for them by herself? He had been so attentive. Had something happened to him! And then there was no sign of either. The plaintive peeps became piteous, right up until darkness fell when, weak and exhausted, the babies must have fallen asleep.

In the morning, the chirps and callings continued – a little weaker if anything. Still no sign of Jenny-Wren. The big, grey, fluffy cat from next door had been lurking about, hiding under a green plastic table cover. Later I fed string through the eyelets and folded the bottom up and tied it tightly around the top of the table, totally exposing the space under it. Horse and stable door immediately sprang to mind!

Back inside, and I suddenly heard a most welcome and familiar sound. It was the chicks' dad, Mr Wren. Sitting on one of the crossbars of the rose arch he put out an urgent call for the hen. He finished his trilling with a couple of pathetic peeps which almost sounded like an afterthought of 'Come on, dear. Where are you?' This was my interpretation as I am by no means fluent in 'Wren'.

He flew to the box a couple of times. I was pleased and thought that the babies were being fed again. Then there was silence. After a while, the feeling of not knowing got the better of me. I parted the twigs again. No little heads filling the opening of the box this time. Had the nestlings actually fledged while I had blinked? Had their mother's absence been deliberate and a prelude to coaxing them out of their safe haven to face the world? I do hope that this was the case, that Mother knows best, and nothing has happened to my lovely little Jenny-Wren.

De-tailed

I couldn't quite make out the dark blob sitting amongst the stems of the pink climbing rose on the fence of the side patio. I could just make out a bit of wing and what seemed like pretty heavy breathing for a blackbird hen, or any hen, come to that.

I busied myself and happened to look out again an hour later. The bird was still in its cage of stems. Now it seemed a little more with it. Clumsily it flew onto the patio and hopped between some flower pots and relative safety. Later I saw it sitting on top of the black umbrella.

Several years ago I had bought a bird feeder station. I was disappointed when I assembled it, as it was much too low. All that is left of it now is the planter with a centre pole into which I have attached the handle of an umbrella and tied it so as not to take off with the first gust of wind. The whole contraption stands on a garden table onto which I put bird food. The umbrella ensures that bread, seeds and food scraps keep dry, and it seems to deter the bigger birds too.

The hen looked like a ball of feathers and was obviously still in shock. It was fluffed up to keep out the cold. The poor thing didn't have a tail feather to its name, and some wing feathers were also missing. Without the primaries, its wings were reduced to mere stubs, more akin to a fledgling's and not suitable for long flights or quick get-aways.

The hen is a resident and one of last year's chicks. If she stays alert among the flower pots and in the vicinity of food and water, I hope that she will gather strength and, who knows, might even get to grow a few new feathers to replace her present great loss.

Bully

A couple of years ago my friend from Australia was here for three months. She loved the garden and swapped between the various benches and chairs, strategically placed in order to follow the sun. Edith took great delight in her surroundings and took the feeding of birds, squirrels and hedgehogs very seriously. If I happened to be in the kitchen, or wherever, I would hear her call, 'There's a hedgehog on the mat, can I put some nuts out, please?'

One night, while one spiky creature was happily having its supper, another one turned up. Straight away it laid into the first one with vehemence and nasty aggression, forcefully pushing it, again and again. In the ensuing battle the first one came off rather badly. It seemed to sustain some sort of injury to one side of its face or snout.

The injured party turned up the next evening, favouring its left back leg and seemingly pushing its right cheek along the ground.

The aggressor returned, and without provocation attacked the already injured party again and again. I wanted to open the door and put a stop to those continuous attacks. However, it was best not to interfere with nature. These two obviously had some sort of dispute to settle. Through the closed patio door I did shout, 'Stop it, you bully!'

Last year, after hibernation, Bully turned up again. Imagine my surprise to find that what we had assumed to be a male was actually a female. A male came onto the scene and relentlessly wooed Bully. Still carrying the previous year's injuries, the other hedgehog was able to eat without any further persecution.

Blacky No-Mates

Not long after I wrote 'De-tailed' I noticed a blackbird with an odd-shaped right leg. When next I saw him it wasn't just his leg, but his foot too was badly damaged – the toes were bent right back so that he was walking on his wrist. It looked awkward and most painful.

He landed on the table to gather food and seemed able to cope, left to his own devices. I didn't think that he would last very long. However, some months later, he is still around. There are some six or eight blackbird cocks flying about the garden and the two gardens either side, right now. If they all sat or stood still long enough for me to count them, I'd get an accurate figure.

No matter what number, they are all chasing after him all of the time. Why? He, with just one good foot, is no threat to the others as regards playing the field of females. I doubt very much if he'd ever be able to balance on a potential female long enough to become a dad. I feel quite sorry for him, because other than his obvious disability, he is quite a handsome little chap and would, I am sure, make a wonderful father.

Chooks

After my earliest associations with chickens as a child and a teenager, later with Hanna in Calabria, I didn't think I'd ever have the opportunity for an affinity with chickens again.

The past couple of years have been dreadful as regards to winter weather. Last year I lost a lot of shrubs and bushes to severe frost and snow. While sowing, cutting and digging the shrubbery, next door's four chickens kept me company. As I dug up a worm I'd pass it through one of the slats of the fence. I tried to be fair by feeding one of these juicy morsels to each in turn.

The other day, I was hoeing and a couple of the chickens kept abreast of me. Hoeing, unfortunately doesn't seem to turn up much in the way of worms. I kept telling the chickens that but they didn't believe me. They continued to ask and cluck, cluck until they eventually went off. I don't think they like me any more!

Looking for Warmth?

There are changes taking place around here. The rooftops of the neighbouring houses, usually reserved for doves, crows, magpies and an odd heron now and again are being sought by blackbirds, robins and tits.

There were four male blackbirds on one roof just now, and sitting close together, at that! Not a common sight as they are usually quite territorial, although it is a bit early in the year to be establishing territory or supremacy. We have endured a long, harsh winter to date, and it is not over yet! Have these smaller birds found warmth on the roofs of centrally heated houses?

During the hardest days of frost, ice and snow, all the birds were conspicuous by their absence. Looking out in the mornings when my car looked like a huge misshapen snowball or a massive car-shaped ice cube, it was little wonder that the birds stayed in hiding – you wouldn't have sent a dog out in that weather!

I was away for three weeks, which didn't do my birds any favours. I started putting food out again, but didn't see one bird even, for quite a few days.

Things are pretty much back to normal now. I am sure that there have been some casualties, but not too many I hope. Like the birds, I too am looking forward to the spring and warmer weather.

The Beauty of the Night

With the sun setting to the right of the garden and daylight fast fading, the first of the bats will flit through the dusk. Soon, it will be time to put out nuts on the mat under the patio door. If it's wet or threatening to rain, I stand a small green garden table over the mat to keep the nuts dry, as well as the hedgehogs while they are feeding.

I like to sit in the dark with just the outside light on. It throws an eerie light across the top garden. The bark of the oak looks silvery grey. Either side of it, trunks, boughs and branches look stark and menacing against the backdrop of the inky blackness. I sit and wonder by what sort of locomotion the moon sails effortlessly through the sky. Then again I wonder, who switched on the stars at night? With all that energy being used I take heart as, even up there, power cuts occur from time to time, especially when it is cloudy!

I am in awe of all around me. When the moths dance in the lamplight, hedgehogs vie for peanuts, owls, camouflaged by oak leaves hoot to others nearby, I too will still be up, enjoying the serenity and drinking in the beauty of the night.

Music to my Ears

A light breeze teased the leaves of bushes and some tall trees around me. It was pleasantly warm, and even hot whenever the sun dodged passing clouds which winds high up quickly pushed along.

The soft June breeze blew an introduction as the wind chimes tinkled like the sound of softly struck tubes of a glockenspiel. Like the sounds of running water, gently cascading, like the glissando as nimble fingers slide up and down harp strings.

More winds gathered en masse and played through the canopy of trees. Boughs, branches, twigs and leaves were aroused and the previously played prelude became an opening to a unique symphony. Leaves and twigs sounded like the gentle notes of violins and piccolos.

The winds gathered strength, and with more and deeper breaths came the sounds of bassoons, cellos and finally the drums as the whole orchestra, led by an almighty musical director, climaxed in a crescendo. Just then, the winds abated and took a breather.

What a wonderful performance of such beautiful sounds of an open-air concert, played just for me, right here, in my back garden.

Memorable 12th of July

I had a busy hour and a half in the garden before lunch, and later in the afternoon, another two hours. I always find it rewarding to stand back and see what I have done. Better still, go upstairs and look down and get an overall picture of a job well done.

A little past dusk, I put out peanuts on the mat under the patio door. Earlier I had replenished the water in the milk cartons which serve as drinking troughs for the hedgehogs.

I noticed the security light above the patio door had come on. I checked, but no hedgehog. One could have come and gone before there were any nuts, or a cat might have set off a light.

It came on again. This time there was a little hedgehog, chomping away for all it was worth. It had obviously not long got up and seemed to have problems with fleas, and fleas, and more fleas. Scratch, scratch and scratch. It pushed its chin and underparts along the mat and across the peanuts to combat the itching.

The light went on again, and then there were three! A male, a female and a little one. The male, feeling very amorous turned his attention to the female, squeezing in between her and the youngster and circling the female, clockwise and anti-clockwise. She made no attempt to get her behind up against the bricks as I had observed so many times before. He repeatedly nudged her sides. It looked as though he was trying to push her over.

After nearly half an hour he succeeded in getting onto her back, piggyback style. He held on tight with his front claws dug into the forest of spines and copulation started. He thrust again and again, with frequent breathers. She lifted her head high, whether by the sexual actions, in ecstasy or pain, who knows? She looked as though she was sniffing the night air.

Copulation continued. I lost count after more than a dozen frenzied thrusts of his lower body. Then she tried her best to uncouple herself by making a getaway but with him still hanging on, hitching a ride. In so doing, they left a trail of sperm on the flagstones. She managed to free herself at last but he followed in hot pursuit, just out of sight amongst the plant pots on the small patio. And there they stayed for about two and a half hours, she all the time snuffling and snorting her objections at any further advances from him.

For over 25 years I have watched, listened to and fed generations of hedgehogs, always wondering how they procreate. Tonight, I watched them in action. So now I know!

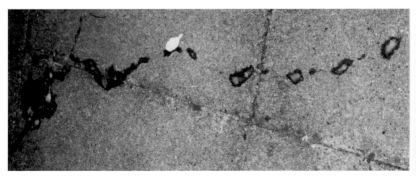

The Last Chapter

Many years have passed since Robin introduced you to his garden, which was the beginning of years of observations and all the changes to and in my garden – years of getting it to how it is now. You wouldn't recognise it. I wish you could see it!

The seasons will come and go. Bushes and shrubs will need to be cut back. Roses will need pruning. Grass will want cutting and tall plants anchoring safely to stakes. And, no matter what, the weeds will always try to outdo me. Snowdrops and crocuses will brave the cold start to each new year and the bluebells will carpet the bottom garden. Roses will bloom from early June 'til Christmas and even into the new year. The stream will continue to flow, gently trickling, or rushing off when swollen by rain.

The patio, down in the dell, next to the stream will remain a lovely, secluded sun trap. A sanctuary to sit and read or just to listen to the birds and the soothing sound of the water.

New babies will arrive each spring and early summer. I have lost track of who belongs to whom. They all came and multiplied. It is safe to say that all the birds, hedgehogs and squirrels are the offspring of those mentioned by Robin and in subsequent stories.

It would be folly of me to keep writing about which birds are building nests and where, or the noisy, lengthy courtships of the hedgehogs and the funny antics of the squirrels.

Around teatime, the blackbirds will have much to sing about especially, in the spring, each one, between several gardens, singing heartily, waiting for the others to respond. Oh, how I wish I could speak 'Blackbird'. I can only imagine what messages they are sending and what news they are telling each other.

I will bless the days when I wake up with the sun. I will love those days, able to sit out and watch closely when it will seem